OFF MARKET REAL ESTATE SECRETS

The Underground Blueprint to Buying and Selling Off Market Deals

By
Jeff Leighton

Copyright and Disclaimer
Off Market Real Estate Secrets
Copyright © 2016 All Rights Reserved
Written by Jeff Leighton

This publication is protected under the U.S. Copyright Act of 1976 and all other applicable international, federal, state, and local laws, and all rights are reserved, including resale rights: you are not allowed to reproduce, transmit, or sell this book in part or in full without the written permission of the publisher.

Limit of Liability: Please note that much of this publication is based on personal experience and anecdotal evidence. Although the author has made every reasonable attempt to achieve complete accuracy of the content in this book, they make no representations or warranties with respect to the accuracy or completeness of the contents of this book and specifically disclaim any implied warranties of merchantability or fitness for a particular purpose. Your particular circumstances may not be suited to the examples illustrated in this book; in fact, they likely will not be. You should use the information in this book at your own risk.

Any trademarks, service marks, product names, and named features are assumed to be the property of their respective owners and are used only for reference. No endorsement is implied when we use one of these terms. Finally, use your brain. Nothing in this book is intended to replace common sense or legal, accounting, or professional advice and is meant only to inform.

First Edition

Table of Contents

Introduction 4

Chapter 1: Finding Investors and Buyers for Your
                Off Market Deals 6

Chapter 2: Finding Off Market Deals 15

Chapter 3: Exit Strategies For Off Market Deals 36

Chapter 4: Analyzing Off Market Deals 50

Chapter 5: What to Watch Out For With Off
                Market Deals 62

Chapter 6: Building Your Off Market Team 87

Chapter 7: The Major Keys To Off Market Success 98

Chapter 8: Negotiating and Submitting Offers 128

Chapter 9: Alternative Real Estate Investing ideas 139

Chapter 10: Real Estate Education, Certifications,
                 and Mentorship 152

Chapter 11: Resources For Your Off Market Business 160

Chapter 12: It Is Your Turn to Start Doing Off Market
                 Deals. 167

Introduction

Over the last several years it has become tougher and tougher to find good investment deals listed on the market. The days of finding discounted properties on the MLS are gone and margins have shrunk to the point where in many markets it does not make sense to buy anywhere near what the homes are listed at if you are looking to do a short term flip or find a significant discount.

In this book I am going to show the exact steps that myself and other investors and agents I know use to consistently find highly discounted "off market" deals that nobody else knows about. These types of properties exist in EVERY market in America and could be yours with the right marketing tactics and tools that I cover in this book.

As an example of the amazing potential with off market deals, as I am writing this I have a property under contract that is not listed on the market at 350K in a great area and the house literally next door, a similar model is listed at 635K and will probably sell at or around 600K. I have worked (and still work) with many of the top off market investors in the country, names who you have almost certainly heard of if you have ever watched any house flipping shows on TV and I have done an estimated 1000 individual consulting and coaching calls with students all over the country on how to uncover these hidden gem properties.

If you are looking to set up a system to get these type of off market leads week in and week out then this is the book for you. You will learn how to access a range of off market homes in your area from single-family homes, town homes, condos, and even vacant land or commercial buildings. I have done numerous off market deals and have seen the amazing potential they have to bring in five or even six figure checks.

I promise that if you follow the steps I lay out in this guide it will not only open your eyes to a world you probably did not even know existed, but you should be able to start closing some of these highly profitable deals.

This book is for any type of real estate professional including investors, real estate agent, lenders, and really anybody looking for good deals in their own market. Whether you want to do just one deal a year or several deals each and every month I show you the exact steps to take to find these off market properties. Take action now and you will be amazed at the type of opportunities you can uncover just by doing the marketing I cover in this book.

CHAPTER I

Finding Investors and Buyers for Your Off Market Deals

Finding investors and buyers for your deals is actually one of the easiest parts of this business. When you first get started, your biggest concern is typically: "where will I find the capital needed to make my first deals?" But, what you will realize is that money is everywhere. Finding the deals is more important. Below are the top strategies for finding buyers and investors for your deals.

LinkedIn

LinkedIn is an amazing resource that can be used to build lists. Let's say you are building a list of real estate investors for Los Angeles, California. All you would have to do is type in "real estate investor" in the search bar for LinkedIn, about 100,000 people might show up, so the next step is to click on "people," then you can narrow it down by the city. Next, go ahead and type in Los Angeles or whichever city you desire. You will get a more refined list of about 1,000 people in the real estate investment industry including rehabbers, wholesalers, real estate agents, hard money lenders, and more.

The next step is to start building your buyers list by going through each name and getting their contact information. Luckily, you can hire someone on Upwork.com for five dollars an hour to build a list like this for you. Some people don't have their contact information publicly listed on LinkedIn, so just tell your virtual assistant to spend a minute or two researching on Google to see what they can find. If the information isn't readily available, that's okay as there are about 1,000 other people on there to seek out. Ideally you want to compile a spreadsheet of at least 250 top buyers and their contact information.

This is exactly how I built my buyers list: by outsourcing the online research. Keep in mind that you don't need to reach out to all of these people unless you really want to or if you have a deal for them. Many people will not respond to you if you cold call or contact them out of the blue, so be prepared for a slight amount of rejection if you decide to reach out to each one individually without an introduction from a mutual acquaintance. This type of list building can also be used for hard moneylenders, wholesalers, real estate agents, or any one else you could possibly think of as being helpful in growing your business.

Google

Google is an amazing resource that investors sometimes overlook. You don't know how many students I speak with who don't have any people on their buyers list. The first question I ask them is, "have you Googled 'we buy houses' (insert your city)" and they say no. Just by Googling "we buy houses (insert your city here)" you will often times find at least 15 to 25 investment companies among the search results.

You can usually tell by their ads and website who is the most legitimate, so this is a good starting point. A more in-depth approach would involve cross-referencing to see which investors are on both the organic ads and the paid ads. Chances are those people have invested the most in their marketing and are a good bet to be the most active. Online research is an easily accessible first place to begin. You can start by organizing a Microsoft Excel spreadsheet with company names, phone numbers, emails, and any other relevant information.

REIA (Real Estate Investor Association) Groups

One of the most obvious ways to build a buyers list is to go to as many networking Real Estate Investor Association (REIA) events as possible. This includes Meetups, REIA groups (each city usually has several), and any other real estate type of event. Just exchange business cards and ask people what types of deals interest them. Very simple!

Remember that many cities have multiple REIA groups as well as multiple Meetup groups related to real estate. What I've found in my years in real estate investing is that some of these groups are extremely well run, while others might be less organized, but if you go in there with a positive and open mind you are bound to learn something. Additionally, some of these Meetup groups may be held at properties that an investor is working on.

Seeing these deals happen in real time can be very beneficial, so keep an eye out for those types of events. These Meetups and REIAs will give you a good sense of what is going on in the market and are also a great place to find referrals. Don't be afraid to ask for referrals at these types of events for title companies, lenders, contractors, agents, and more. You will never know the outcome if you don't ask!

Working With Other Wholesalers

Here is a sneaky way to build buyers list. I stumbled upon this approach after having seen it happen to me several times and then I developed it into a more refined strategy. This is how it works, once you get started in the off market world you should try to build the largest list of wholesalers possible.

This will help you in several ways. First, they will send you deals that you can practice evaluating and possibly even find a great deal through them. Another great thing about getting on a lot of wholesalers lists is that some of them are not very tech-savvy and when they send you a deal they may forget to blind carbon copy their buyers list. You don't know how many times (probably once a month) a wholesaler will send me an off market deal and will CC (carbon copy) like 500 other people. You can then just add those people to your buyers list.

A few words of advice, don't spam people and only send out a deal if it's yours and you are sure it's a good deal. I was once networking with another investor friend of mine and he said this email gift happens in his market as well. He even has a name for it, "the motherload strategy," where a wholesaler or even a real estate agent might accidentally CC their entire buyers list to you when they send you a deal. If they do happen to send you a list, be mindful of its value and keep it as a resource for when come across a great deal.

Partnerships or Joint Ventures

If you are in desperate need of a buyers list or investor for one of your deals, a strategy I have used in the past and continue to use is to leverage established wholesaler's buyer's lists. The first wholesale deal I ever made was accomplished using this strategy. If you have a good deal but you don't have enough buyers yet you can contact another wholesaler who you know and trust and get them to send your deal out on their buyers list.

You typically only want to use this strategy with a veteran investor who knows what they are doing because there are implications if it is not done correctly. You have to sign a joint venture agreement with that investor, usually no more than a page long, just to show that they are now technically in control of the contract. You can't just contact 10 wholesalers and tell them all to send out your deal without an agreement because you can get in trouble with real estate agent boards over that. There is a local investor in my area that I partner with where if I get a deal that I am not sure about I send it over to him and he blasts it out to his 10,000 buyers (yes, that many) and it's almost like we are just listing the property on the market. Usually the fee associated with sending it out on another wholesaler's list is a 50/50 split.

However, everything in real estate is negotiable and in some areas I have found it to be lower, sometimes about 25% of the deal. For your first couple of off market deals I would recommend this strategy and think of it almost like training wheels. Find the top off market specialist in your area and partner with them in some capacity on your first three deals or until you have a good understanding of how they work.

Hard Money Lender Strategy

A bonus strategy is working with hard moneylenders. Not all hard moneylenders will do this but the smart, open-minded ones will. Hard moneylenders will typically have more buyers than ANYBODY else because that is how they get paid. So what you can do is send your deal to them and see if it's something one of their buyers might be interested in. Then the hard moneylender can lend money on the deal as well as get a wholesale fee. You probably need to reach out to five to 10 hard moneylenders to find the one or two that would be open to this strategy.

Some hard moneylenders are still stuck in the "old school" way of lending money where they think they are essentially "god" and that you must bow down to them. It is unnecessary to work with these people. Many hard moneylenders these days are open to partnerships, wholesales, and rehabs. Some of them even do coaching and mentoring.

You will be surprised how many of your competitors are actually open to joint ventures. Some of my so-called competitors actually offer to lend me money, wholesale my deals, and even partner 50/50 on some deals. Try to keep an open mind so that you can leave with the best, most profitable, and win-win exit strategy. Once you get experience as an off market investor you can even evolve to the point where you are doing hard money lending or joint ventures on different off market deals that people bring to you.

Are You Really Real?

One of the most frequently asked questions I get is "how to tell if someone is an experienced or real buyer?" In any major city there are probably hundreds if not thousands of people who say they are "cash buyers." Such a title is not really that big of a deal anymore, since everyone pretty much is a cash buyer. There is no sense bragging about being a cash buyer since most people are, although it is a fact worth mentioning when working with a seller.

The first way and most obvious way is a proof of funds. Now if you are dealing with a person you haven't done business with before it would be wise to ask them for a proof of funds. If you know that they are an established investor you can still ask them for a proof of funds, although sometimes people can get offended by that question. The second way to tell if they are a legitimate buyer is doing some online research. Most investment companies whether they are large or small will have some type of online media presence where you can verify that they are who they say they are.

You can look at their reviews online and see what you can find out. The third way to tell if they are a legit buyer is by doing networking and finding out first-hand who the top buyers in the area are. Once you start going to networking events like REIAs and Meetup Groups you will start to hear the same names over and over again and chances are those are going to be the top buyers in the area. A bonus way is to keep your eyes and ears open for radio and TV ads. A lot of times, only the top buyers in your area are going to be able to afford a marketing medium like that so if you hear their company name, write it down and let them know if you come across an off market deal that you would be looking to sell off.

Story

The first deal I ever put under contract I sent out to my investors in the area and nobody was interested in the deal. I was terrified, here I had this $250,000 property under contract in a great up and coming area and nobody was responding to the deal I put out. Some claimed it was overpriced while others just weren't interested. So what I did was I reached out to a wholesaler in my area and asked him about the property. He told me it was a good deal and not only that but he would send it out on his list and see if we could get any buyers. That is exactly what ended up happening and a couple days later I met five buyers at the property and one guy made me an offer on the spot that I could not refuse. The moral of the story is that I found out I could work with my so-called competition and leverage other people's lists if necessary.

Conclusion

There is no reason not to have a huge buyers list or at the very least 25 or so qualified active buyers in your area. Building a buyers list is something you should be doing proactively, so you have it before you need it. You never know when an amazing deal is going to come across your desk and you need to have all the top buyers at your fingertips so you're not scrambling for a buyer last minute. Either build one yourself, find a local wholesaler who you can work with to send out any deals, or hire a virtual assistant online for five dollars an hour to build one for you. There is no excuse for not having some type of buyers list and this is one of the first things you will need in this business

Action Item

Go on to Google and type in "we buy houses" for your city and build an Excel spreadsheet of the top 25 cash buyers in your area. This is very simple and can be done in any city or state - even Alaska (I just did the search there). Remember that quality is more important than quantity when you are getting started. I remember when I first got started I had like 2,000 people on my buyers list, but was continually selling my houses to the same two or three people. Try to find the sharks in your area first, these are the people buying five to 10 houses a month, and then go from there.

Also, if you have liked what you read so far I invite you to take the next step to get additional resources on the off market world including cool training videos, updates, live coaching, and more. All you have to do is text **OFFMARKET to 444999** to stay updated on everything going on in the off market world.

CHAPTER 2

Finding Off Market Deals

This is my favorite chapter of the book. We are going to explore how to find off market deals and offer more than 10 proven strategies you can steal from me. I only ask that if you implement what I talk about and start doing deals that you please send me some testimonials! The idea behind any of these marketing plans is taking massive and decisive action, i.e. putting up two Craigslist ads a day is not going to cut it. You need to think like the Dan Kennedy quote where you are "doing so much marketing that if you haven't offended someone by 12 noon each day you probably are not doing enough." And if you don't know who Dan Kennedy is I would look him up ASAP and get a copy of every book he has. We will start with the most practical and proven strategies and get more advanced from there.

Old School Direct Mail

Direct mail is going to be your best source of leads for finding off market deals. I repeat, your best! The reason behind this is that most people do not have the patience or ability to send out direct mail on a consistent basis, which gives you a huge opportunity to market to motivated sellers without a ton of competition. This source of leads is also going to be inexpensive (fifty cents per postcard, one dollar per letter).

    The key with direct mail is to build a list (or buy a list) of potentially motivated sellers and then market to them at least three times over the course of six months. Building the list and sending out the mail should not be taking up too much of your time, this is a marketing plan that should be put on autopilot with you managing the process maybe directly spending an hour of your time on it per week. I use an online program called RealProspect 2009 to manage when I need to send out my direct mail, however there are plenty of services available that can track your mail. The way it works is I upload my list via an Excel spreadsheet and then RealProspect alerts me every 45 days when I need to send out my next mailer. When you have multiple direct mail campaigns going this makes it much easier to manage everything.

    Keep in mind that with direct mail your response rate is going to be anywhere from 1% with postcards to maybe 5% if you are using personalized "yellow letters." Most investors are going to mail a small list once, maybe get a call or two and then get discouraged and never mail again. This increases the value of your mail because as you continue to send mail, you competition probably has given up. Some of my best deals have come on the multiple touch campaigns.

    Your best direct mail lists for finding off market deals are going to be from motivated sellers. You do not want to just contact everyone in the neighborhood. A quick example of this is a nail salon that just opened up in my area. Instead of choosing their market carefully i.e. women of a certain age who would be more likely to use a nail salon they send their marketing out to everyone, including me. They could easily sort a list of the most likely prospects, but they chose just to market to everyone and waste money. Some examples of motivated sellers for real estate are going to be probate, eviction, absentee owned, or tax lien properties, among others. Almost all of these lists are available to buy online, or you can go to the local courthouse and find this data and compile the list once a week. Ideally you would outsource this list building process to someone if you do not decide to do it manually.

Bandit Signs

Another marketing strategy I have seen work with great success are Bandit Signs. The first thing is to make sure they are legal in your area! Call your county code department or look online. These are not the most glamorous, but they can be a great source of leads. The idea with this campaign, and most others, is to set up a system where you outsource the process to someone.

An example system that you could use with bandit signs would be to put out 100 signs a month, 25 a week, and have the 25 mapped out on Google maps high traffic areas in low to median income areas where there tend to be more investment deals. Then you take the process a step further and pay someone to put out those signs for you and have them take a photo on their camera of each sign that is up (25 total) so that you don't have to drive all around town making sure they are up. You can even partner with another company (e.g. we buy gold, fitness, furniture) that is putting up bandit signs and split the cost with them since they already have someone putting up signs. With bandit signs since they are not as targeted you are going to get all types of calls.

However, out of 10 phone calls from bandit signs there should be at least two or three motivated sellers. Bandit signs are one of the most proven strategies since you see them in almost every city in America and they are a great way to get started in this business. I have seen some investors even take it a step further and put up large bandit signs on the houses they are working on in the neighborhood letting everyone know that they bought the house and are looking for more.

Wholesalers and Bird Dogs

Wholesalers or "bird dogs," in your area can be a great source of deals. I know some investors that rely almost 100% on wholesalers bringing them deals. A wholesaler or bird dog is someone who does marketing for good investment properties and then sells them off market to other investors at a discounted price. The way to make it work with wholesalers is to build a list of them and remain in constant contact. If you just have one or two wholesalers sending you deals you probably won't find too many options.

You also need to think of wholesalers as any other type of lead, by that I mean for every 10 leads they send you, there might be one or two potentially good properties in there. Most of their leads are going to suck. Wholesalers are notorious for sending over properties that they massively overvalue or where they undervalue the cost of necessary repairs. You don't know how many times I'll get a deal from a wholesaler who says the entire house just needs $10,000 of repairs, when that is not close to the real estimate of work the property needs.

If you were to build a list of maybe 25 or so wholesalers and email them once a month asking what they have available, the chances are that their combined efforts may yield one or two great deals. The great thing about wholesalers is that this is a free source of leads and can add to your deal flow. I know one investment company that actually has a Meetup group where they attract hundreds established and aspiring wholesalers and train the wholesalers on what exactly to look for in a deal and how to send it to them to evaluate. You can even wine and dine your best wholesalers so that they send you the deal first before blasting it out on their list.

One way to build a list of wholesalers is local REIA groups, Meetup groups, and networking events. Or you can just go on LinkedIn, type in "wholesaler" then go to "people", then go to your local city, and make sure "real estate industry" is selected, and if you live in a major metropolitan area there should be a list of at least 25-50 wholesalers. You can also call bandit sign numbers and get their email address because a lot of times those will be wholesalers.

Door Hangars and Door Knocking

Door hangars and door knocking is another great strategy that can be implemented by anyone and is also a great way to learn your neighborhood. If you are on a very tight budget then I would recommend door hangars or door knocking. You can buy 1,000 flyers at your local print shop for dirt cheap. I'm not sure how these print shops even make a living it is so cheap.

Then during your lunch break, weekend, or whenever you have free time you can go door-to-door with these. If you live in an urban area you can get up 40-50 in an hour. If you did that every day for one hour and put up 50 every day during your lunch break, five days a week equals 250 a week, which equals 1,000 a month. I can guarantee this will generate calls coming in.

Door hangars are similar to direct mail so you could expect somewhere around a two to three percent response rate from those. If you put out 1,000 a month that would equate to approximately 20-30 phone calls each month. There are some door hangar examples in the back of this book if you want to get started with those. This is also a strategy you can outsource to a neighborhood kid looking for a few extra bucks each week. For this strategy you want to find a neighborhood where there is a lot of investment activity and lots of cash transactions. Any local real estate agent can look up the hot zip code where the most cash transactions took place over the last year and that would be my recommendation on where to start.

Pay Per Click (AdWords)

Pay Per Click ads are one of my favorite marketing tactics. This is a more advanced strategy that I wouldn't recommend unless you've had some training in online marketing. There are dozens of books on the subject you can buy for $20 on Amazon that are great. I would recommend the author Perry Marshall. The great thing about AdWords and Pay Per Click is that most people do it so poorly and waste so much money that there is an opportunity for someone with just basic fundamental AdWords skills. I know some very smart real estate professionals that have tried this approach and given up since they were just winging it with no real strategy. You would be shocked at how many smart professionals will literally just try to do their own ads without doing any research whatsoever into how the AdWords system really works and how make the most of it.

A lot of these books and/or online articles and courses have 10 simple steps to optimizing your campaign which can easily put you in the top five percent of online marketers. The idea with marketing is that a potential prospect should see you everywhere. Maybe they get your postcard, then they go outside and see your bandit sign, then they go online and see your online ad. Think of it like a military strategy: air, land, and sea. You want to come at your marketing with as many angles as possible. The great thing about AdWords is you can set your budget as small or as high as you want.

Some people I know start with $30 a month and then scale it up to thousands of dollars per month once it becomes profitable. Remember, you only have to pay when someone clicks on your ad. Google has now added a function to detect if one of your competitors is just clicking on your ad to waste your money, so you don't need to worry about that. Since this is such a valuable skill there are companies and other small businesses that will even pay you to run their campaigns if you get good with it. AdWords is transferrable skill to most any type of business.

Call Fire and Cold Calling

Call Fire is another amazing marketing resource. Okay, I must preface this with the acknowledgement that there is a national no-call list. Therefore, I advise consulting with a lawyer before attempting this very aggressive marketing strategy. There is a service, Call Fire, where you can call something like 20,000 people per month. If you were able to do that and your response rate is only minimal you would still be able to generate a ton of great deals. I know of one investor that uses this service and does very well developing leads.

This is another strategy that you could outsource since it's most likely not worth your time to call that many people. The great thing about Call Fire is that it allows you to effortlessly call a full list of people. There are many people available on UpWork.Com that are overseas or in the U.S. that would not mind calling. All you have to do is give them a simple script and train them on what you are looking for and this can be a great way of digging up leads. Be prepared for a lot of rejection! However if you were able to contact 20,000 people in one month and only 10,000 answered their phone, and 9,500 said they were not interested, you would have still potentially 500 people per month who you could make a deal with. If you even converted one of those people then this strategy could make the investment worth it.

Meetup Groups

Meetup groups are another popular tactic for finding off market properties. I know some investors who actually sponsor Meetup groups to teach other investors and real estate agents how to bring them deals. Basically what you do is build up a list of real estate agents, wholesalers, other rehabbers, and anyone else that might be interested in real estate and put on one hour trainings once a week at a local hotel or meeting place where you cover how to find deals on a small budget and, more importantly, how to send those deals to you so that you can add more to your pipeline.

One investment group I know has almost 500 people in their Meetup group and they train other investors how to funnel deals to them. To attract people to these events make sure you are adding a lot of value with the content you will be covering as well as providing free food in a nice location. I've attended some Meetup groups in shady hotels with a handful of people and flickering lights, while others have had 100 people in upscale hotels. I don't need to tell you which is better. If you do decide to start your own Meetup group you should research and visit the other ones in your local area and see what you like or dislike about them. Then based on that, you could create your own "master" Meetup group.

Working With Real Estate Agents

Real estate agents are another great source of leads for off market deals. Before I go into depth on this strategy keep in mind most real estate agents are not fans of the investment industry and probably will not help you out. That being said there will be some, maybe five to 10 percent, who understand investing, how to find deals, and how to work with investors. Those are the ones you will be looking for. You will have to sift through a lot of real estate agents to find the ones that you can work with.

This strategy was borrowed from a friend of mine who worked for a very successful investor who got almost all of their deals from real estate agents with access to off market deals. Here is what you do. First, compile a list of every real estate agent in your market area. Then you go through and call, email, text, whatever you want to do and let them know that you are an investor looking for fixer-upper deals and tell them that if they bring you deals then they can be your buyer's agent, as well as the listing agent on the backend once the property is fixed up. This two for one proposition is very attractive for a real estate agent and should motivate them to find properties for you.

My friend's boss always had a steady pipeline of deals to choose from because there were approximately 50 real estate agents scouring the city looking for deals for him at any given time. Keep in mind that this is only 50 out of about the 5000 real estate agents in that market area, and even that small percentage can be effective. Combining this approach with a wholesaler team and direct marketing can make for a very potent combination.

The "Open House" Strategy

Open houses are another strategy for finding off market deals and let me explain. When I say open houses I don't mean what you are probably thinking where a real estate agent puts up some balloons, a couple signs, and then sits in the kitchen for 3 hours checking their Facebook on a Sunday afternoon. What I am talking about are strategic open houses where you put on free trainings.

One investor I know has a genius strategy of bringing in more deals, more money, and more buzz for his business. What he does is he holds once-a-month free trainings at houses around the area that he is working on, or in other words an "open house". Before he starts the rehab work he will blast out to his buyers list advertising a "free training" and will take attendees through the process. He details the scope of the work, projected profit, how he found the deal, how he's financing the deal, etc. at the event. Usually there will be at least 25 attendees.

During the one hour training he will go over how to send him off market deals, how to partner with him, how to lend him money, and more. This is actually how I met him and since then we have partnered on numerous deals and continue to work together. He typically also holds a training once the deal is fully renovated so that you can see the before and after.

Additional Marketing Theories

Below are some additional ideas that I haven't personally mastered, but may have a lot of potential.

Craigslist

Craiglist is one of the easiest strategies to implement for off market deals but also one with a low ROI. So I only included this because students ask me all the time about craiglist. This should never be a core part of your marketing. If you go on there every day and put up a couple ads on "we buy houses" then at best you will get a couple calls a month and probably mostly from other investors. Craigslist is great for searching for used stuff to buy but do not make this a core principle of your off market marketing. You can get off market leads but because there is such a low barrier to entry I would not focus on this type of marketing.

Mass Texting

Mass texting is a newer strategy that I have seen work very well for different businesses. If you can cheaply build a list of phone numbers from the white pages of a certain zip code or even FSBOs, Zillow "make me move," Craigslist, and any other source then you have a group of people to start marketing to. Even better if you can get a list of motivated sellers such as absentee, eviction, or probate contacts. Since these people probably get bombarded with calls, your text needs to offer some type of value or different angle. My brief experience with mass texting (using Phone.com) went fairly well. I got 70 messages in one day. It was a mixture of some good leads and some bad. I would not recommend using Google Voice for these types of messages because it can lead to you getting banned from their service (ask me how I know ☺).

Dog Walkers

Talking to dog walkers is apparently one of the best strategies to find off market deals. When I was doing additional research for this book I came across an agent who claims to be the off market master at real estate. He told a reporter that talking to dog walkers is one of the best ways to find deals. I haven't tried it, and I am pretty sure he has never tried it. However maybe if you were to go stalk all of the dog walkers in various neighborhoods and offer to pay them per lead generated maybe you could grow this into a viable strategy.

Retargeting

Retargeting is a newer marketing principle that you have probably seen but not realized it. The way retargeting works is that you can put a code on your website that follows anyone that visits your site. So if they come to your site and then start browsing somewhere else, your ad will pop up on different places around the Internet following them around. This can be a great strategy if you generate a lot of traffic to your website and is something I would recommend you look into. This has probably happened to you in the past where maybe you were looking at a pair of shoes to buy on Amazon. Then, a couple days later you might be on another website and all of a sudden you see an ad for those exact shoes you were interested in. That is retargeting.

YouTube Advertising

YouTube ads are becoming more and more popular now and are DIRT cheap. If you want to spread your message further you can create short one to three minute videos about real estate. YouTube videos are fairly easy to edit and produce and there are many editors/producers on sites like Upwork.com that can inexpensively create these videos for you. YouTube ads are also extremely inexpensive so you get your message in front of thousands of potential sellers for about 5 cents per view.

Radio

Radio is another medium that is popular these days and, although I have not tried it, I often hear other real estate companies on the airwaves. It can be expensive depending on what time and channel your radio spot is on, but if you have a decent sized marketing budget I would suggest looking into it.

Search Engine Optimization (SEO)

Search Engine Optimization (SEO) is another type of marketing that is popular and I will tell you how it can apply to the off market real estate business. SEO is basically where you optimize your online marketing for keywords such as "sell house fast" or "we buy houses." I think it is a sublevel marketing strategy that should be coordinated within your overall marketing plan, but not the first thing that you work on. In my opinion, most of your off market leads are going to come from offline activities such as direct mail, bandit signs, wholesalers, real estate agents, and door knocking.

However, if you have a powerful offline campaign going and then you add SEO that can be a powerful marketing strategy. There are entire books and courses, as well as plenty of free information online written about SEO, but here it is in a nutshell. You want to model what other successful companies have done in other cities to rank high on Google. Type in "we buy houses" for different cities and see what sites or web pages are ranked highly. Then you can use those as the blueprint for SEO in your own city. The thing with SEO is that it doesn't happen overnight like AdWords. However, if you have a consistent strategy with SEO you can get ranked highly after a few months and start getting leads that way. Once Google acquired YouTube it has made YouTube videos a more valuable source for boosting SEO rankings.

Social Media Marketing

Does social media marketing work for finding off market deals? As far as I have tested and from the masterminding I do with other investors and agents I do not know of anyone finding off market deals on a consistent basis from any social media channel. Most people are finding them through the tried and true methods of direct mail, bandit signs, networking, and more recently with AdWords pay per click advertising. I think social media is great for building up your brand, finding private money lenders, and testing new marketing ideas, however it should not be your main focus if you are looking for off market deals.

That being said, I think one of the great things about social media is that people are still experimenting with marketing and testing new strategies and seeing if it is possible to find off market deals with consistency on social media. If you are the person that cracks the code on finding off market deals on social media please let me know so that I can update this chapter!

Car Graphics

There is another marketing strategy out there that is easy to implement and has been tested successfully around the country. That is the putting "We Buy Houses" graphics on your vehicles. Now there are a couple ways to do this successfully which I will go over. The first way is just to pay for car magnets (not expensive) and put them on your vehicle. You see these done by investors and it is a very simple way to generate leads.

Another strategy I have seen is investors paying for their contractors to have these magnets or graphics on their cars while they are working on your houses. I have not tried this personally, but I know several investors who are successful with this strategy. A third way is to purchase a large cheap truck and park it in a highly trafficked area with a huge "We Buy Houses" graphic on the side of the truck. If you can find a willing gas station, parking lot, or side of the road that gets a lot of traffic then you can potentially have your ad in front of thousands of people each day. I know one investor who negotiated within the lease with their landlord to let her park a massive truck with graphics in the parking lot of a large shopping area so that all passersby could see her ad.

Contacting Properties That Are Already Under Contract

Another strategy that I heard recently at one of the mastermind meetings I attend each year with other investors across the country was as follows. The investor contacts agents who have houses currently under contract and lets them know he is a cash buyer and if the deal falls through for any reason he might be interested. As a result of this strategy he has agents calling him all the time about deals because it is not uncommon for deals to fall out of contract.

It happens much more often than you would think and for many different reasons, people get cold feet, home inspection items come up, financing falls through, etc. When one of their deals is looking like it might fall out of contract, these agents will often times contact an investor directly letting them know the situation and the investor can take it from there if they are interested. This is not a strategy that you should rely on as the only source for your business, but it can be a great supplement to your monthly lead flow. Most investors do not do this, which means less competition, too.

Air, Land, and Sea

You should think of your marketing like a military style attack via land, air, and sea. I wish I could take credit for this analogy but I believe I got this idea from marketing legend Jay Abraham who I would advise you look up. With air, land, and sea marketing you are not dependent on just one source of leads. For example, a lot of investors and real estate agents usually just have one source of leads like referrals, or using the MLS to find deals, or Facebook ads.

You should ideally have three sources so that if one dries up your business is not dead. Think of a barstool, it is a much more solid platform on three pegs than just one. Some examples from my own business was that I used to only do direct mail, and I was (and still am) very good at that source of leads. However, soon after getting my direct mail systems set up I then started doing a lot of online marketing to bring in motivated leads. Now I have a third source of leads, referrals from agents, investors, and others I have met throughout the business.

Your three sources of leads do not have to be the same as mine and you don't necessarily need them next week, but continue to work to build them. There is a real estate agent in my area that has the air, land, and sea marketing down perfectly. In the morning sometimes I will walk across the street to the coffee shop and I will see her "coming soon" and "for sale" signs all over the place. Not only that but I might see a bus that goes by and on the back of the bus I see her information and advertisement. She is already the first person I think of when it comes to real estate in my area and then when I come home chances are I probably have a piece of mail from her.

I have seen that she does significantly more than just those types of marketing and I am sure with the range of the net she is casting, she will be getting a lot of deals from it. The air, land, and sea strategy is a long-term strategy that should be the goal of any business. Play to your strengths when it comes to bringing in new leads but also explore new avenues of lead generation. There is enough information out there to learn how to dominate whatever form of marketing you choose.

Thomas Edison Style Tests For Marketing

I love marketing and love trying new things, in fact, if I am not trying some new form of marketing each month I get a little restless. Think of your marketing almost like you are a scientist in the lab testing numerous variations of different experiments. Most of your marketing efforts probably won't generate the amount of calls or deals you are hoping for. However, by taking massive action and doing lots of marketing tests you can "increase your rate of failure" and find out which ones actually do work. Remember, not everything will be a success but it is only a total failure if you fail to learn from the process or the outcome. Besides, doing marketing tests can be a lot of fun and a break from your normal routine.

Sometimes you will get great responses; sometimes you will get people calling you out on YouTube saying how much you suck (ask me how I know). Conducting marketing tests makes you a more skilled marketer and sometimes implementing a marketing program will lead to some other marketing idea that you had not even considered before. The best marketing tests to do in my opinion for off market deals or whatever it may be is to model and deploy.

For instance, one marketing campaign for off market deals that I have only talked about 100 times in this book would be a direct mail campaign to motivated sellers like probate, absentee owned, eviction, etc. Or another could be starting a YouTube channel modeling (and improving) a channel that you really enjoy. Another option may be an AdWords campaign based on something you bought online recently, and the list goes on and on. The faster you test your ideas to see which ones work, the faster you will find the diamonds in the rough. And once you have two or three highly optimized campaigns going on each and every month then you will have a steady stream of leads and can cherry pick the best ones for your deals.

If you want to be doing one off market deal a month you should be in contact with at least 50 different prospective sellers. Keep that number in mind: 50 leads = 1 deal. This is a rough estimate I was provided by a mentor early on in my career, and my experience has found it to be fairly accurate. By increasing the amount of action you can find out which marketing plan or system is the home run much sooner.

Joint Venture Relationships

One way to open your business to more deals and more profit is the way you see your competition. I talk with investors and real estate professionals from all across the country and no matter if they are in Los Angeles, California or Des Moines, Iowa they all say that their market is very competitive. Here is a new mindset for you to consider that will open up a whole new possibility of deals: think of your competitors as potential partners.

What I mean by this is that the real estate industry is not as cutthroat as people make it out to be. Many of your so-called competition could actually become private moneylenders for you, find off market deals for you, or even be partners on joint venture on projects. Everybody is looking to do more deals and sometimes that could mean that your competitor could lend money on one of your deals where they make a good interest rate and you get a loan that is less expensive than hard money. Or maybe one of your competitors has too many deals going on and they don't want to take on another project, so they could wholesale to you one of their deals and make it a win-win for everybody.

When you see your competition as potential partners instead of competition it opens up a whole new world of possibilities for deal making. To learn more about creative joint venture possibilities I would look into the marketing mogul Jay Abraham and especially his book called "Getting Everything You Can Out of Everything You Got."

Story

I was working with one student who told me he was going broke with his marketing and I asked him what he was doing. He told me he had paid hundreds of dollars each month to be on shopping carts in some grocery store. I immediately was shocked and confused. Why would a new student on a tight budget run off and pursue an unproven marketing strategy like that? I don't mind trying new marketing ideas and I don't even think that shopping cart marketing is a bad idea, but why would that be your FIRST marketing plan? Well, he didn't have this resource to guide him! Start with the proven stuff (direct mail, bandit signs, wholesalers) and then once your budget allows for it, do whatever your heart desires.

Conclusion

The best advice I can offer you is to start with one marketing campaign to get some leads. You should only try proven marketing campaigns when you are getting started. It's not the time to be creative. There will be time for that later if you execute the proven strategies. Then scale up so that you are generating at least 50 leads a month. I made a game out of it after I was told by a very successful investor that if I wanted to do at least one off market deal a month I would need to make my phone ring 50 times.

The reason for that number is that 75% of your leads will be non-motivated people. They are just looking for an offer, but have on intention of making a deal quickly. You do not need to spend time on those leads. You will only spend time on the 10 out of 50 or so leads that are motivated. These are the folks that tell you, "I need to sell my house ASAP," "I do NOT want to use a real estate agent," and/or "the house needs a TON of work." Think of your marketing like an all-encompassing strategy. Six months from now you want your marketing surrounding prospective leads from all angles. Ideally you want to have three solid, steady forms of lead generation all coming from different sources (e.g. direct mail, online, and networking).

Then you take it a step further and put someone in place to run your marketing and you get to a point where you can cherry pick the best deals. I know one investment company that has scaled up to the point where they get over 500 leads a month (and do over 100 deals a year). Don't think that you need to be on that level, you can do great with just getting 50 seller leads each month and still find great deals!

Action item

Choose one, just one of the marketing plans we talked about above, steal it from me, then deploy it. You only need to start small, just get something out the door. I started by sending out 25-30 letters a week and getting a few leads here and there. Learn how to get five leads in a month, then 10, then 50, etc. Every person has different strengths and weaknesses. I found that I love direct mail and it works for me. Maybe you are different though and you are the computer expert and can get online leads, or maybe you are the networking king and can make use of your charisma and people skills, or maybe you are old school and like putting up signs. The key is to get something out there and get started!

Also, if you have liked what you read so far I invite you to take the next step to get additional resources on the off market world including cool training videos, updates, live coaching, and more. All you have to do is text **OFFMARKET to 444999** to stay updated on everything going on in the off market world.

CHAPTER 3

Exit Strategies For Off Market Deals

In this chapter we are going to do an in-depth exploration of the multiple exit strategies for off market properties that you have as a real estate entrepreneur so that you can make best use of each deal you come across. There are seven different profitable strategies below, almost all of which I have used. I will share my experience using each strategy with you. During this section try to think of yourself as a transaction engineer not just a real estate agent, wholesaler, or rehabber. More exit strategies means more opportunities for profit!

Buy The House For Yourself

I know it sounds simple. It may even sound greedy, but if you are actually doing marketing for off market deals you will sometimes come across properties that are perfect for you to move into, fix up, and offer you instant equity. I have kicked myself a few times for passing up on some of these deals. I remember when I first got started there was a beautiful two bedroom, two bath condo on the top floor of a building in the heart of the city views of famous landmarks and close to the baseball stadium.

This would have been a perfect place to move into. I was new to the off market business, so instead of keeping it for myself I wholesaled it out to an investor who did a great job fixing it up and selling it for significantly more. It was nice at the time, but I wish I still had that property now! If you want to, you can even target your marketing more specifically to the actual areas where you would want to live, although I prefer to market more towards motivated sellers. If you need to finance an off market deal and you only have a couple weeks to get it closed, then look to hard moneylenders. They can be great resources for your off market deals and will get you the cash you need quickly. Usually they lend on six-month terms, in which case you can re-finance at a later date.

Fix Up Or "Rehab" The Home

This means you find the off market deal, you put money into renovating and then you sell for a profit. This is probably the riskiest strategy although also has the highest upside in terms of profit. I would only recommend rehabbing if you have done some investment (wholesale) deals in the past or if you have a background in construction.

One way to tell if it's a good deal or not is to ask your hard moneylender. These guys are often a good resource because they have dozens of investors a day sending them deals and they usually only approve one or two percent of those offered. So if you're not sure it's a good deal, ask a hard moneylender and get a second opinion. You always want to use the MAO

(Maximum Allowable Offer) formula when evaluating deals, which is "After Renovated Value" times 0.7 minus the cost of repairs, or in other words MAO = ARV X 0.7 – Cost of Repairs. This will leave you enough of a margin for profit, overruns, and fees associated with closing.

Always plan on the rehab taking a little bit longer than you expect and costing a little bit more as well. If you really qualify and only find the best rehabs to work on all you need is two or three of these deals a year to achieve good results. Just keep in mind that you are looking for the top 0.1% of deals, and if you have enough marketing going out you can find the diamonds in the rough.

Wholesale The Property

Believe it or not, in the investment world and the off market world, this strategy happens all the time. Most real estate agents have never heard of this strategy or will tell you it's illegal. Feel free to ignore them. This is when you find a house that is off the market and you get paid an assignment fee for bringing it to another investor. For example, I am working on a deal right now where I am looking to put it under contract for $92,000. I know an investor who pays around $115,000 for these exact types of houses. If I fix it up and sell it for $270,000 I might be able to make around $70,000 net profit, however that does not come without risks and may take six months from start to finish. In this case I might just send the deal over to him and make a quick $15,000 profit in three weeks instead. This shorter timeline and quick sale can be a great strategy if you have limited time, need a quick cash infusion, the house needs more work than you're comfortable with, or don't yet know enough about construction and repairs.

This is the lowest risk strategy and can be a great way to get started in real estate investing. I almost always recommend doing three wholesale deals before your first rehab so you can get a better foundation and learn what kinds of deals to look for. Once you get to a point where you are getting lots of leads you can wholesale out the ones you are not sure about and cherry pick the best rehab properties.

Be The Buyer's Agent On The Deal

If you are a licensed agent, which I would recommend if you are going to be in the real estate industry, you can be the buyer's agent and listing agent on off market deals. The way it would work is if you find an off market deal you can tell your investors about it and they would pay your buyer's agent fee for the deal. You would not charge this to the seller. Your buyers will love you for bringing them an off market deal at a discount. Most investors would also give you the listing on the back end if you are bringing them these great deals. This can add double the deals to your pipeline.

Prehabbing A House

A fifth strategy for off market deals is one that not too many real estate agents, investors, or others really know about. The strategy, prehabbing is where you do some light work to the house so that it is more prepared for when the rehabber comes in to do renovations. It is a step beyond wholesaling and a step before rehabbing and can be a great strategy to use if you are looking for a faster return, but lack the capital to risk getting wrapped up in a construction project.

With prehabbing you typically want to at the very least remove all trash or debris that might be in the house or the yard. Many off market houses I have been in are sometimes littered with garbage, so just the step of "taking out the trash" can make the property look much more attractive to any rehabber. Also, with prehabbing you are typically picking up the house off market and then listing it on the market, which increases your potential buyer pool and may mean that you can fetch a higher price for the property. Typically with prehabbing it's going to have to be a cash buyer to purchase the house, although sometimes the home is in good enough condition to be financed conventionally.

This is one of the easier exit strategies when it comes to off market deals since you are really just finding a great deal, doing a minimal amount of work to prep the property, and then listing it in the "as is" condition. Although you may not realize it, this strategy happens all the time. Just look in the listings in your area of "fixer upper" type of houses and I can guarantee you at least some of them are investors who found a great deal and just got the property cleaned up and ready for the next investor. I remember I sold a house to an investor for $110,000 that also involved the sale of a piece of land right next to it. A couple of weeks later I see the same property listed on the market in "as is" condition for about $60,000 more. The investor made a killing on it and all they did was remove debris and trash from the house.

Work With Another Investor

A Sixth strategy is partnership on the deal. There are many ways to partner on off market deals if you are not sure what to do and you have a great lead on a property. One way is to partner on the rehab. If you put a great property under contract you can reach out to experienced investors in the area and ask if they want to partner on it with you. Usually that would mean that all you have to do is bring the deal and the investor will supply the funds, contractors, and experience in getting it completed. Sometimes you may split this arrangement 50/50 however most of the time the investor bringing the money, contractors, and experience will get 75% and you will get 25%. However, the experience you are gaining is invaluable.

This can be a great strategy if you are new to the business, you want to learn the rehab industry, and/or you don't want to have a ton of risk. You can watch the process unfold before your eyes, get paid, and learn a ton. Some hard moneylenders are also willing to partner on deals since they see 100 houses a day and know what a good deal is. A lot of times these hard moneylenders want testimonials and case studies to show off on their website. Therefore, they are always looking for newer investors to work deals with and showcase.

Another form of partnership that I have used is partnering on wholesale deals. Basically the way that works is you find a trustworthy wholesaler with a huge buyers list (think 10,000). There is an investor in my area and probably in every major metropolitan area that have huge buyers list. Basically you can have them send out your deal to their buyers list and if you have a partner with a large buyers list it's almost like your listing the property on the MLS. You set up an appointed time for any potential buyers to view it and then select the best offer. This is a great strategy because you will have more eyes on the house, which means potentially higher price and you are partnering with an experienced investor who has done this before which means the chances of your deal going through are much higher.

Refer The Property

If you are very new to the business and you think you have a good lead or two on your hand then simply refer it to an agent or an investor. By now you should have a list of investors, real estate agents, and other real estate professionals that are in your local area. Look online to see who seems to be the most active and legitimate and pass the lead on to them. Maybe you'll get a referral fee, maybe not. It depends on licenses and legalities but at the very least you can get some feedback on whether or not it's a good deal.

One strategy for investors is to send all of your unqualified leads to an agent and have them work on it. If you are generating 50 or 100 leads a month strictly doing investing there's only a couple of those leads that are going to be profitable for you since most of the people will want retail price. What you can do is give the list of the retail price people to an up and coming real estate agent who can then market to them and try to get a deal then possibly give you a referral fee.

Or if you get a short sale lead you can send that to a short sale real estate agent and they will love you for it. Have a list of different experts in your area that you can send leads to that you are not sure what to do with. Many times if you are sending people great deals then they will want to reciprocate either in the form of referral fees, assignment fees, or other great perks like free basketball tickets or dinner.

Become A Transaction Engineer

One of my mentors, Ron Legrand, has one of the best ideas on real estate that I have ever heard. In your off market real estate career and in general you should strive to become a transaction engineer. What I mean by this is that you should not just limit yourself to off market deals or just being a real estate agent or just doing rehab properties. I know plenty of people who have gone their entire real estate career by just doing one thing like only being an agent, only being a wholesaler, only being a rehabber, and on and on.

By learning these different exit strategies you can maximize your profit on any leads that come your way. Once you start doing off market deals you have a minimum of three exit strategies. You can be the real estate agent on the deal and bring a buyer, you can wholesale the deal, rehab the deal, or perhaps even buy the property as a long-term rental. Starting out as a real estate entrepreneur I left a ton of money on the table by not understanding and leveraging these different exit strategies. I can remember countless properties where I would have made much more if I was the agent on the deal, if I had wholesaled the deal, or in some cases with my off market deals if I had rehabbed or even held on to these properties and used them as rentals instead.

The top earners in real estate are those that have a good understanding of every exit strategy and maximize each lead that comes in. Most people are not willing or able of learning additional exit strategies so this can give you a huge advantage in your market.

What Is The Next Level And How Do I Get There?

You should always be thinking about evolving your skills and business. "What is the next level and how do I get there?" That is a quote by one of my favorite entrepreneurs Eben Pagan, who is big on evolving your business. It is amazing to me how many real estate entrepreneurs' businesses are exactly the same every year. In my opinion, you should always be learning new strategies, testing out new marketing plans, and evolving your business to the next level. Like Eben Pagan says, and I am paraphrasing, no matter where your business is there is always a next level and it is somewhat arrogant to think otherwise. It is not even about creating more work or hiring more people, maybe you want your business to evolve to the point where you are doing less work.

The point is continued evolution. The top entrepreneurs I know in real estate are always expanding their minds by going to seminars, reading books, attending mastermind events and are hungry for success. I talked about this in an earlier part of the book, but part of getting to the next level could be adding services to your business, creating marketing systems for your business that save you time, or any number of things. The possibilities are endless.

How Easy Are YOU To Work With?

One thing I aspire to and a thing I look for when I'm working with other agents, investors, and professionals is how easy are they to work with? You want to gain a reputation of being an easy to work with professional who does what they say they are going to do. Some people in the business will be very difficult and you should avoid these people. I worked with one real estate agent who is constantly in legal battles of various sorts and he even told me the only reason he went to law school was because "he gets sued a lot." That is an example of a red flag and someone to stay far away from, and not surprisingly he has a terrible reputation in the business. The higher you move up the ranks the easier I have found it is to work with people. One company I know that specializes in off market deals is very easy to work with and I will give you a couple examples of why: They are fast and responsive, since they know with off market deals they are not going to last forever.

    I remember specifically working with someone else who seemed unable to send an email under 1000 words. It was like everything was an essay and then they would actually get mad when people did not read the long confusing email messages. Even speaking with this person was difficult since they tried to make everything sound as corporate as possible. On the other hand, this company I do business with will have quick and straight to the point messages and they personally care about those they do business with, so there may be a little small talk as well.

Another point that ties into the theory of being easy to work with is doing what you say you are going to do! If someone or a company says one thing and does another then that is a definite warning sign. In this business you cannot afford to have delays or people saying one thing and doing another. The first time it happens, give them the benefit of the doubt, but if you start to see a pattern you should seek to avoid working with them. Look for the positive, reliable, and easy to work with type of people. They are out there you just need to find them.

How To Present Off Market Opportunities

When you come across a great off market opportunity at a discount there are a couple ways you can present your deal to your investors or clients if you decide you want to sell it. The first way, if you are a real estate agent is to get your client to pay your buyer's agent commission and send their offer to the seller - pretty simple stuff here. That is only after talking with the seller and getting a strong confirmation that that price is going to work.

If the deal is a really good deal, which many off market deals can be, then you might want to have your buyer let you list the property once it is renovated. This is more of an aggressive tactic so it won't always work. Usually when I present my deals to investors or clients I will have several photos (about 10, if I can get photos) and then I will also have a brief description of what work is needed and what I think it can sell for. I know some people that will give only the purchase price and after renovated value, while others who have a whole entire novel about the property, history, etc. In my opinion, the best way is somewhere in between giving your client just enough info to make an informed decision but not too much to overwhelm them. If you are an investor you can put the property under contract and maybe even send it out to your list if you are undecided on rehabbing or wholesaling it.

Occasionally, if you are not sure it is a good deal or not you can even find the top buyer or two in your area and just shoot them a quick message about the deal you are working on. They can usually pretty quickly tell you whether its worth it or not, the top buyer is often times not going to need a ton of information. So to wrap this part up, pictures are great (see if there are any previously listed photos of the house as well), in addition to a brief description of the work needed and the after repair value. Any good investor is going to run their own numbers anyway, but it is helpful to have them know your opinion on the property as well.

Is Staging Worth It?

Any renovated house that you sell I 100% believe that it should be staged. I can't tell you how many buyers have no vision when it comes to houses and think some rooms are so much smaller than they actually are. With furniture a house can take on a whole different life. A good stager can help you sell your property quickly and for the most money. I remember I even took a two-day class on how to become a stager. Not because I actually wanted to become a professional stager, but because I wanted to learn how to properly set up a house for the optimal experience.

There are countless books, articles, and courses you can read or take out there on staging, but basically it comes down to de-personalizing the house, de-cluttering the house, and adding green features such as some plants. There is an art and a science behind staging and I would recommend paying for a well-established stager, because staging gone wrong can just be straight up embarrassing. I have seen some stagers or want-to-be stagers use old dusty furniture from the garage. You want to use a professional company, not a weekend stager unless you can see some examples of their previous work or get a referral from a trusted source.

Story

When I first got started in the business I was a one trick pony for too long. I only did wholesale deals. I got pretty good at finding discounted off market houses from motivated sellers. My investors loved me, they would wine and dine me, ask me to work for them, etc, However, what I realized is that I was leaving tons of profit on the table by only having one exit strategy. I learned that it's more important to be a well-rounded real estate professional with various exit strategies that can maximize your profit and minimize your risk. At this point in my career I can wholesale, rehab the houses of my choice, list properties, and represent an investor buyer as an agent. I really believe that the sky's the limit. At any given point I might be doing any combination of these things at once. I wear different hats to ensure multiple streams of income.

Conclusion

I see it everyday, most wholesalers have no idea how to rehab, most rehabbers have no idea how to wholesale, and most real estate agents don't know how to buy off market deals. Generally speaking, almost every real estate professional I see is leaving heaps of money on the table. Like the legend Ron Legrand said, you need to become a transaction engineer. Think versatility.

As a former college basketball player sometimes I like to compare basketball to real estate. Think about Lebron James, he is not a one trick pony. He can rebound, score, dish out assists, shoot, and even get steals. Or think about Draymond Green for example, a player on the Golden State Warriors. I saw him play in college and I thought there was no way could this guy make the NBA. I thought he was fat, slow, short for his position (6'6" power forward), and couldn't really shoot. Fast-forward several years and this guy is on his way to a maximum-level contract and is one of the best players in the game. He worked on his abilities and can do all of the aforementioned things fairly well. He is never going to lead the team in points or rebounds but he regularly fills up an entire stat sheet since he is so versatile. He doesn't have any glaring weaknesses that are holding him back. Most NBA players, like real estate professionals, have just one specialty, but if you can expand into different niches you will be much better off. I can guarantee it.

Action item

Start learning about the different exit strategies mentioned above and visualize yourself doing them. There are plenty of case studies and examples of these types of deals available via interviews on YouTube by BiggerPockets, FlipNerd, and many others. As you start to get more and more off market leads some leads may be better as a rehab, wholesale, agent deal, or even buy and hold. I don't want you to miss out on some of the profitable exit strategies available because you didn't know how to handle them. The highest earning off market real estate professionals do it all.

Also, if you have liked what you read so far I invite you to take the next step to get additional resources on the off market world including cool training videos, updates, live coaching, and more. All you have to do is text **OFFMARKET to 444999** to stay updated on everything going on in the off market world.

CHAPTER 4

Analyzing Off Market Deals

Analyzing off market deals is very important and you must have a system for doing so. In this chapter we will talk about a good rule of thumb for evaluating deals, as well as what to look for in selecting them. When you first get started in the real estate business you think everything is a deal. You need to be able to have a system for picking only best deals instead of just finding the average priced houses. It is better that you are very picky about deals instead of just doing a lot of deals with little profit potential. I knew one company that chose some deals "just to stay busy," knowing that they were not even going to make a profit. I don't know about you but I would rather do one deal a year that makes $100,00 versus five or 10 deals where you make a small profit on some, break even on others, and lose money on the rest.

MAO (Maximum Allowable Offer) Formula

The best rule of thumb for analyzing deals is the MAO formula. This is a commonly used term in the investment industry for rehabbing properties, which stands for Maximum Allowable Offer (MAO). The way it works is you take the after renovated value multiple that times 0.7 and then subtract for the cost of repairs and then you get your maximum allowable offer. Ideally you want to be under that number although sometimes you can even be above 0.7. In the case of a small project with a quick turnaround time in a great neighborhood you can sometimes go above the 0.7 and still do well.

However, in a neighborhood that you are not sure about and a house that might need extensive work you want to be more conservative and probably go in at 0.6 or 0.65. This gives you enough room for profit, closing costs, and any overages. If you are looking at an off market deal for your own personal residence or as a rental then you can obviously go above the MAO formula. The key is to stay below what the property would typically sell for on the MLS so that you know you have some built in equity. Also keep in mind that most houses you look at are not going to be at the MAO formula, most will be above that, sometimes by a significant margin. The MAO formula also only applies to condos, townhomes, and single-family houses, not parcels of land. But if you do come across a deal that meets the MAO formula, you need to move quickly.

Zillow Evaluation

If you do not have MLS access and you are new to real estate a couple of resources you can use are Zillow or Redfin. Keep in mind this is not going to be an exact science, but if you have a motivated seller and you know price they are looking for you can compare that with the Zillow/Redfin value. You typically want to see a significant discount in what they are asking and what the value is. A lead I am working on the seller verbally agreed to $92,000 and the Zillow/Redfin value is closer to $270,000. Keep in mind this house needs a complete gut rehab, but this is just an example.

In some cases it might make sense to actually pay around the Zillow/Redfin value if the neighborhood is super hot and there might be a potential for new construction, condo conversion, or major addition. Again, this is a rough estimate, but if you have a motivated seller that wants to sell as soon as possible, the house needs a lot of work, and the Zillow/Redfin value is significantly higher than what they are asking for then that could be the deal you are looking for. When you are getting started in real estate Zillow and Redfin are great to look around to get a general idea of what properties in different areas are selling for.

Deal Analyzer Tool

The best way to evaluate deals is by using the deal analyzer: Many hard moneylenders have deal analyzer calculators on their websites which make it easy for you to come up with potential profit. All you have to do is plug in the estimated repair costs, estimated after renovated value and what you are purchasing the house for and the calculator will do the rest. Many new to real estate ventures think that if you buy a house for $300,000 and put $50,000 into it and sell it for $400,000 then you have a profit of $50,000. Sometimes naïve sellers will even call me with their property claiming that if I buy it at $200,000 and put $50,000 in to sell it at $300,000 then I would make $50,000 net profit.

It is very important, especially when starting, out to rely on a deal analyzer this will save you time and headaches. There are even deal analyzer apps that you can download for your smartphone that will give you an estimated profit. At the back of this book are a lot of valuable resources for your real estate career including a deal analyzer that you can practice on with properties in your area. Once you start plugging in numbers you start to get a feel for where you need to be at in terms of price in your area for it to be a deal of any significant value to you.

Qualifying Leads

Ok this is a very simple metaphor, but think of your leads coming in like you are searching for gold in the Wild West. The way it works is that they have a machine in the water that brings tons of dirt, pebbles, etc through a conveyor belt and then at the bottom most of the stuff gets discarded and there are a few gold pieces that come out. Your leads are going to be the same way - most will be garbage. By that I mean most of the sellers will want retail price, they will want the price that the house would sell for if it was listed, however they don't want to pay a real estate agent commission. I have sellers all the time that say I'm just curious just make me an offer, and in those situations it is usually a non-motivated seller. That is okay because for every 10 leads I get there are usually a couple "gold pieces" or motivated sellers.

The motivated sellers will tell you I want to sell immediately and the house needs a lot of work. It's even better if they are absentee owned and the house is vacant. When you are starting out you can practice evaluating all the deals that come in however once you get cooking you should only focus your time on the motivated sellers. For every lead that comes in for my business we take the sellers through a lead interview sheet which has basic questions like address, condition of house, bedrooms/bathrooms, etc and can give us a good idea of whether the seller is motivated or not. This conversation with the seller should only last for a couple minutes just to build a little bit of rapport and get the basic property information. Some sellers will want to tell you the history of the house and any number of other things, but your time is worth money so keep the conversation short.

Deal Or No Deal?

If you are unsure whether your lead is a good deal or not here are a couple options. First make sure that the seller is motivated and make sure there is some type of discount between what they are asking and the Zillow/Redfin value. The next step is to reach out to either a local investor or hard moneylender that you trust and ask for their opinion. If they are an active investor they will get back to you quickly and let you know. Obviously if you ask them about the deal you should probably give them first priority if it's something they are interested in.

What I see often is a lot of wholesalers and real estate agents will send out deals to me and other investors without having done any type of qualification whatsoever. This is obnoxious because it's almost like the boy who cried wolf. I have one wholesaler who just sends me deal after deal and then I'll look the property up and it's either listed on the MLS or it is way overpriced. This guy even calls me from different numbers now because I just started ignoring his calls. Make sure you qualify your deal and then AFTER you qualify the lead, if you are still not sure about it, then reach out to a local investor that you trust.

Outsourcing Your Way To Success

Eventually what you want to do is outsource your lead qualification. This can be done a couple ways. Number one there are plenty of live answering services out there for small businesses including PAT Live, Answer First and more. All you have to do is give them your seller interview script and then anytime someone calls you will be notified with an email or text about the lead and then its up to you to follow up and convert. Eventually you can get an acquisitions assistant or lead manager who can qualify all the leads to you so that you are only working on the motivated sellers.

This can free you up to come up with new marketing campaigns and other income generation ideas while freeing you from answering the phone every 10 minutes with a seller. I have seen many investors and agents do it in different ways, some will use an answering service, others will answer the phone directly, some have an assistant that takes calls, and others have every lead go straight to voicemail. I have seen the business work in all of those scenarios, however the most important thing is getting a lot of leads. If you are only getting a couple of calls each month, none of these strategies will work.

Understand Your Zoning Laws

When evaluating deals, Understanding the zoning laws is something that sounds boring but can actually be exciting and immensely profitable. Each county and city has different laws in regards to zoning that are often widely available online on the county's site.

I would read and study these zoning laws when you have some free time because it can help you out when it comes to exit strategies. Furthermore, most other investors and real estate agents have very little knowledge of these. Here are a couple examples of how zoning laws can add significant profit to your deals. In many urban neighborhoods and cities there are zoning laws that allow rowhomes to be converted into multi-unit condo projects. So, depending on the zoning code and square footage of the lot of the property you could turn a single rowhome into three, four, five or more condos and sell for hundreds of thousands more. It happens all the time.

I know one guy who got very creative and was able to make a substantial six-figure profit from this strategy. What he did was buy a property that did not quite meet the zoning requirements for building condos since it was short by about 300 square feet based on the size of the lot. Since he was a contractor by trade he offered to build a $25,000 deck for his neighbor in exchange for them deeding him the 300 extra square feet he needed to build condos.

As a result of doing that he was able to see a substantial amount more on his profit on the back end. Another example is with single-family homes; sometimes they are actually zoned to allow for two, three, or even four townhomes. By knowing these laws you could potentially see profit where others don't. I have also seen some neighborhoods where it is almost impossible to build a new house because of certain designations and zoning requirements. I would advise becoming very comfortable with your area's zoning laws so that you can maximize each property you come across and see potential where the majority of others won't.

The Types of Properties You Will Encounter

When it comes to off market properties, this entails single-family homes as well as condos, land, townhomes, and even commercial properties.

Single Family Properties

Single-family homes are usually the easiest to evaluate and are the most common type of off market deal. One thing to watch out for with single-family homes is smaller houses. For whatever reason a neighborhood might have a couple houses that were built significantly smaller than the other ones. By that I mean the house might only be 800 square feet or smaller.

The seller will want significantly less than any of the comps, however keep in mind that re-selling these types of properties can be very difficult. I typically stay away from homes under 800 square feet unless I have three solid comps that show me that people buy these houses and at what price. Also houses that are right on the busy road or have unusual lots will typically sell for less than the comps so make sure to factor that in to your estimated value. That being said, there is a price for everything. I would purchase a 700 square foot house in front of a fire station, in a bad area for the right price; you just have to be very conservative.

Condos

You will also come across a lot of off market condo deals, especially if you live near a big city. There are a couple things to watch out for with condos. The resale value of condos can vary drastically depending on what side of the building the unit is facing, what floor the unit is located on, the square footage of the unit, and if the unit comes with a parking space.

For example, there are often times one-bedroom or two-bedroom condos that vary significantly in square footage even within the same building so you can't always just take all the one-bedroom condos and use those at comps. You have to take it a step further and find the similar square footage and ideally a similar floor condo that sold recently. A top-level, one-bedroom penthouse condo is going to sell for more than a ground level, one-bedroom condo.

Always try to reach out to the condo board or management association to find out the process for renovation. Usually it is not going to be a big issue since renovations are common, but you want to have as much information as you can going into the deal. You should try to become the expert on any building that you are going to be buying in. Often times you can either call the board, talk to the front desk person, talk to a resident, or do some basic online research, and you can become an expert on the building in no time.

Townhomes

As far as townhomes go, this is going to be similar to single-family homes. What you need to look out for with townhomes is what the end units sell for versus what does an interior unit sell for? Also, some townhomes within the same community will have a garage space while others may not, so watch out for that as well. Does your townhome back up to a park or back to apartment buildings? The comps will be different depending on what is behind or in front of your unit, so make sure you are comparing apples to apples when you analyze a townhome deal.

Raw Land

When it comes to land this can be a very profitable off market strategy, but you have to know what you are doing. Look at the zoning in your area, read about it, and try to be informed on land use before attempting one of these deals. For this type of transaction you need to partner with an experienced investor who has done land deals before. They are very different than a standard single-family house deal because some land you can't develop unless it's a certain size, or maybe you can develop it into three townhomes instead of a single-family home. I would only work with your most experienced investors on this one and I would not buy land yourself unless you are very educated on the land development process in your area.

Historic Districts

There are some parts of town in my area and probably yours where the property might be in a historic district. This is usually a good thing if you come across an off market deal here because that means the price is probably going to be a lot higher for resale value. A couple of things to keep in mind with these is that any renovation work is going to take much longer to go through architectural review boards and what not and will probably be more expensive as well.

Often times with historic districts, you have to keep the exterior of the house looking the same or very similar to the original design of the house in the 1800s or whenever it was built. That means you may have to find more expensive materials to match the house to keep with the historic guidelines. I would not let historic districts scare you away though. Some of the most expensive houses can be found here and most of the time you are still allowed to do plenty of interior renovations as long as you keep the exterior the same. Each city has different codes and guidelines for their historic properties so I would go online and do a little research on the guidelines for your area. This information is oftentimes readily available on your county's website and is also actually pretty interesting stuff and can give you a competitive advantage when selling the home.

Story

When I was first getting started in real estate investing I had no idea there were actually deal analyzers out there. We were purchasing houses almost willy nilly just looking at deals and seeing there was a big difference in the purchase price and potential resale price and going from there. This can (and did) get me in a lot of trouble. You need to know exactly what your potential profit is going to be including all the costs, fees, and time it could take to sell a property. The actual price that you have to buy houses at to make a safe profit after renovation is going to be much less than you first expect when you get into this business. That is why I like using hard money calculators because they are conservative and always see the worst-case scenario.

Conclusion

If you don't have a system for analyzing deals then you are at the mercy of the seller. I would advise using a combination of the MAO formula, deal analyzer, and also making sure that any deal you sell or buy is below (ideally significantly below) what the house would sell for on the MLS. When you are running your deals you also do not want to project that the value of the house could be higher than the comps. You have to rely on sold properties, not some theory you have that the economy is going to go up (or down). If you still have questions about your deal the best practice is to ask a hard moneylender or an investor friend. Hard moneylenders are usually pretty cynical (in a good way) and most of the time only want to lend on deals if they are a slam dunk. The bottom line is that if a hard moneylender thinks it is a good deal then chances are you have yourself a winner.

Action item

Start practicing sample equations on the deal analyzer, find a hard moneylender and use their deal analyzer for different houses that are for sale in your neighborhood. You will be surprised at what prices you actually have to purchase houses at to make a good profit. Here is one that I like to use and you should practice with http://bit.ly/2dcJwQW.

Also, if you have liked what you read so far I invite you to take the next step to get additional resources on the off market world including cool training videos, updates, live coaching, and more. All you have to do is text **OFFMARKET to 444999** to stay updated on everything going on in the off market world.

CHAPTER 5

What to Watch Out For With Off Market Deals

I have seen a lot of off market deals since getting into real estate and making this niche my specialty. Below are the top things to watch out for when you are doing off market deals. Learn from my mistakes and read this chapter twice so that you can avoid some of the mistakes I made when first getting into the business.

Make Sure Your Repair Estimate Is In The Ballpark

When I first got started investing in real estate I had no idea how much houses cost to renovate. My partner and I would take a guess at how much houses would cost and this got us into a lot of "tight" deals. This is very important to understand because sometimes someone else will send you an off market deal and tell you that the house only needs "x" amount of work to make it brand new. They could be right (though usually they are wrong), but if you just went by what every wholesaler, real estate agent, or investor told you then you could end up in a lot of trouble.

The best way to figure out repair costs is to look at case studies of other deals. Here is a great place to get started http://bit.ly/2eiQKCO. You should also join your local REIA as well as any relevant real estate Meetup groups. Often times at these groups, they will go into detail on exactly how much it took to repair the property, how long it took, issues they ran into, etc. You need to be very conservative when you first get into real estate investing, there are also many repair estimator calculators online and elsewhere that I would recommend using.

You can even practice on your own house, neighbor's houses, etc. Keep in mind with repair estimators you are never going to be 100% on the exact dollar amount of repair work. What you can't have happen though is to be off by a large margin. I usually add 10% to whatever number I come up with in terms of repairs and you always want to look out for major, unexpected repair items. For instance I made an offer on a property one time that had a massive tree root pushing against the foundation of the house. I didn't think it was structurally affecting the house, but boy was I wrong. The basement wall was completely bending from the force of the tree. Fixing a foundation wall is easily $10,000, if not $15,000 or more and that was not something I had included in my budget.

I had to renegotiate with the seller in the end since this was an unexpected cost. We actually got the deal done but it would have made things easier and more profitable if I had pointed out the foundation repairs needed in the beginning to the seller.

Speed Is Key

Another huge mistake is SPEED. You typically need to move fast in the off market world. This is not the MLS where you have a first time homebuyer looking for a townhome in a neighborhood where there might be 100 different options for you that all look exactly the same. With off market properties as soon as you get that motivated seller lead you need to evaluate the property and if it looks like a good deal, make an appointment to see it or make a verbal offer to the seller over the phone if they are not local.

I know one investment company whose motto is "we will make you an offer in 7 minutes or less." That is fast! I mentioned this briefly earlier, but when I was starting my investment career I got a call over the weekend from an absentee owned property. I could have called him back that Saturday afternoon, but instead I waited until Monday called him and the property was already under contract. I found out it had sold for an unbelievably low price and the seller had just gone with the first offer since they wanted the deal done as soon as possible.

The moral of the story is that with off market deals, typically the seller is looking for the fastest, easiest, most hassle free sale possible with price being number four or five on their list of priorities. If you are the first one in the door and make a fair offer then often times you can be the buyer. You don't know how many sellers have called me and told me they are going to go with me only because I was the first card they got. Soon after losing that first deal I became almost paranoid about being the first one in the door. I also diligently follow up on all leads. I constantly picture other investors moving in on my territory, which motivates me to be the fastest and most efficient out there.

Garbage Deals

Don't send out garbage! Many wholesalers and real estate agents will send out deals that are not really deals. If you are actively looking for off market deals be sure to do your own evaluation of the deal and not rely on a real estate agent or wholesaler. It is better to send out only one or two deals a month that are actually deals rather than sending over junk every other day.

Wholesalers and real estate agents will often times tell you that the house only needs carpet and paint, or only $10,000 in repairs and then you can fix it up and sell for $1,000,000. It happens all the time so just take any lead with a grain of salt and let them know that you are going to be doing your own evaluation of the property as well. That being said, if you are sending out a deal ensure you are conservative in your estimates. It's funny how I sent a deal out to a local investor and he was so used to being sent awful deals that when I sent him this deal and actually ran the numbers correctly he was completely shocked to be contacted by a real investor. Now when I send him deals he responds quickly since he knows I'm a professional and serious about my business.

People To Avoid In This Business

This may sound obvious, but there are some additional people you must avoid at all costs in this business to be successful (in addition to the aforementioned idiots) and those are people with substance abuse issues, people doing shady things, and the "know-it-alls" who have not actually accomplished anything substantial.

Throwing Idiots To The Crocodiles

As one of my mentors Tai Lopez says, you should "throw the idiots to the Crocodiles". There will be some lawyers, wholesalers, real estate agents, and even title companies that are unaware of the investment or off market world. They might not know what an assignment fee is or are uncomfortable with all cash closings, etc.

You need to only work with investor-friendly people. We once had a lawyer at a title company who told me wholesaling and assigning a contract was illegal and that we couldn't close there. Since closing was just days away we let our end buyer know that they were in breach of the contract if they didn't close and that there are plenty of other title companies that can get the job done if their title company was unwilling. We ended up closing at our title company and it was actually funny the lawyer was still trying to sabotage our deal.

When a title company or real estate agent or lawyer is used to seeing the same type of deals, conventional financed, using a real estate agent, etc and then they see an off market, assignment deal with cash it can throw them for a loop and they don't understand. In the world of lawyers and real estate agents not understanding something can sometimes automatically signal them that it must be illegal. Rely on the trusted, experience network that you have built if you are confronted with this situation.

Drug Addicts

At one point early in my career I worked with a highly successful agent and investor who was addicted to prescription medications. He was a functional addict and did well on the deals he was involved in. However, there was a dark side. I endured working on deals where my partner suffered emotional breakdowns, was accused of crimes against others, and many other things that were damaging to our business and personal relationships.

One specific instance that I recall was his friend that he just recruited on to our team showed up one day with rashes on his skin, a vehicle completely damaged from what looked like an accident on the way to work, and eyes completely bloodshot. While this was all troubling, it could have been even worse and resulted in a serious legal and liability issues for all parties involved since he was technically part of our team. He also brought on another person who had similar issues and would show up an hour or two late everyday, complain about working together, and would argue with our contractors and other people.

It was not exactly an ideal working environment to say the least. Fortunately, I was able to extricate myself from the business relationships and I learned a valuable lesson early on. I share this part of my early career in real estate because I hope that others our there will not have to endure the toxic work environment that I did, even if it was just for a short time. There are enough successful people in this business that do not come with unnecessary baggage, so there is no reason to work with those that do.

Is Someone Being Shady?

Shady investors, agents, title companies are another group of people to watch out for. For your first off market deals I always recommend partnering with a top local investor in your area. To find them all you have to do is Google "we buy houses 'your city'" and do a little online research and it should be pretty obvious who the top buyer in your area is.

The way you partner with one is to start marketing and find some qualified leads, and only send this top investor your best, most qualified cream of the crop leads. They will love you for it and should be able to buy your deal as a wholesale, you can be their buyer's agent if you are licensed or if it is a really good deal then sometimes they will partner on the rehab with you. The reason to partner with them is to learn the right way to do deals and avoid costly mistakes. In the off market real estate business just like anything there are going to be some shady characters out there.

I used to run into them all the time but not so much anymore since building my "dream team." A top investor will be able to guide you through the process of doing an off market deal and you can watch them complete your deal in real time. You might not make as much when you partner with one of the top buyers since they usually have high standards for their deals but you can be sure that the deal will be getting done. I have had investors try to go behind my back to get my deal, I have had agents try to steal my deals, and I have had title companies try to rip me off with high fees. When you work with an experienced investor they will show you the best people to use in the business, who to avoid, and you can use their same resources after getting a level of comfort and "taking the training wheels off."

The Know It All

The third type of person, probably the most common, is the "know-it-all" who claims to know everything there is to know about real estate, yet has not actually done any of the things they are giving advice on. They may even be successful in their own right. However, if you sense close-mindedness and/or arrogance it may be best to avoid working with them until you gather more information.

They will be a thorn in your side and there is not much hope for teaching an old dog new tricks. Once this person has learned real estate the way they learned it and seen some success, they might not be open to off market deals. I know one real estate agent in particular who can give you 1000 reasons why you should not invest in real estate (although now he claims to be the off market specialist), but this guy has done maybe one investment deal in his entire career.

This is not the type of person you should be seeking investment advice from. Always keep in mind who you are getting your advice from and whether or not they are actually practicing what they preach.

Liens That Come Up

Ok with off market properties, a lot of times you come across properties that are typically paid off from a mortgage standpoint, but might have massive liens on them for a variety of reasons. I have had properties with child support liens, delinquent condo fees for over five years, car payments, you name it there has probably been a lien for it. Keep in mind that this is almost normal with some of these motivated sellers and that most liens will not stop you from closing the deal.

After you get a property under contract and send it over to your title company they will be the ones responsible for finding any liens owed on the property and letting you and your seller know. Most of the times with the off market deals I have done what happens is that the seller just gets less money than they were originally going to get. The bottom line is that you should not flip out if you come across liens, they will happen and typically they are not going to derail the deal. Just make sure you have a good title company that has been recommended to you by another investor or two.

The Top Myths Of The Off Market World

Let's talk about some of the top myths that investors, agents, and others will tell you about the off market world and the real estate business in general.

No More Deals Available

This is my favorite because ever since I got into the real estate industry in 2010 it seems like I hear this every year. It is hilarious because most agents and investors will tell you that the best time to do deals was always "last year." Almost always, these are agents and investors who are not being strategic whatsoever in their marketing efforts and are relying solely on over priced deals listed on the MLS.

They will tell you these types of discounted off market deals don't exist and, again, they are sadly mistaken. They say that because they personally have never done it and if they tried they may have had a bad experience, so now they go around telling the world their theory from their singular experience. Furthermore, they are often times not evolving their business in any way. By that I mean if you are an investor who knows and understands real estate and you can't find any deals to rehab, why not offer to lend money to the investors who do find the deals?

In that case you could still make a five-figure profit and still be directly involved in the business. Or maybe if you are a real estate agent you start doing direct mail prospecting to bring in leads outside of fixer uppers on the MLS? There are countless ways to adapt and evolve.

Are Off Market Homes Illegal?

Sometimes real estate agents and others may think that buying a wholesale deal or off market deal is illegal or unethical. I have seen it happen many times where if a deal is not done exactly the same way that the Agent did their last 10 deals with conventional financing, listed on the MLS, then it can throw them for a loop.

What they don't realize is that not everyone wants to use a real estate agent. Some people would prefer to not let the whole world know their house is for sale, some want to sell in two weeks, others just want the most hassle-free sale. Price is not always the number one factor in selling as hard as that is to believe. According to Prevali and other real estate sources about 20% to upwards of 40% of properties that are sold never actually hit the market, so don't let some supposed know-it-all try to tell you differently.

Too Much Competition

Everyone markets to off market motivated sellers so there is no more opportunity: Some agents and investors will like to tell you that everyone is sending them postcards, door knocking, and doing online advertising, so there is no room for anyone else. This could not be further from the truth.

Regardless of how competitive a market is and how many investors there are, as long as you have a steady stream of leads (at least 50 a month) from the right type of sellers then you will be able to find deals. Some of my best deals have come from sellers who told me they received numerous other letters, but someone else didn't answer their phone or mine was the first postcard, etc. If you stay consistent with your marketing (e.g. 3-5 touch direct mail campaign) you can find deals in any market.

Think about the successful growth of Starbucks. When they first got started as a business in the 1970s there were coffee shops everywhere and people were wondering why anyone would think it would be a good idea to open yet another coffee shop. Starbucks' marketing set them apart and yours can too if you follow the marketing strategies I outline in this book. There is always room for a good marketer in any market. Don't worry about your competition. Focus on sharpening your marketing skills.

FSBOs Versus Off Market

Off market deals are always the lowest priced: While this is usually the case, there are properties called for sale by owner FSBOs. These are most of the time "off market" although they are typically priced anywhere from 10-20% higher than any other house in the neighborhood. These are not houses I would typically market to or even consider an "off market" deal because almost always they are so unrealistically priced that there is not enough profit margin to be worth my time.

There was a real estate agent I knew who liked to brag about the thousands of off market deals he has access to, however what he was referring to are FSBOs, or in other words some of the most non motivated people in the business. This is not what we mean when we are looking for off market "deals" unless you are looking to convince gullible people of your abilities. Off market deals typically come with significant discounts on price, so stay away from FSBOs.

Dangerous Houses

You should not buy off market deals with mold or structural issues: This is a more advanced topic here and I will go into a little more depth shortly, however some of the best deals out there might have mold or possible structural issues. Now, to buy or sell these types of properties you need to either be very experienced or have an investor who is experienced that can take on this type of property. 95% of the buyers out there are going to be scared away by those issues, however if you know how to estimate the cost and scope of work you can factor that into your price. I knew one investor who used to love moldy houses because he could get a huge discount and would just come in with a mold remediation team after closing and eliminate the issues.

Another thing to watch out for with off market deals are the moldy homes. Should you buy an off market house with mold? More often than not, when you are working in the off market business you will come across some gnarly houses. You will have houses where hoarders lived, trap houses where drug dealers set up shop, as well as houses with water damage. Now, for the novice investor or homebuyer seeing or smelling mold in a house is a complete deal breaker. However, you should not let mold derail your deal.

Always take proper precautions including using a mold mask if necessary and try not to stay in a moldy house for too long, but keep in mind that a lot of times mold and water damage can be remediated. I remember I sold one water-damaged house that had mold growing around the entire first three inches of the house from a flood that happened a while ago. Since my investors were completely gutting the house and doing landscaping and grading work as well this did not bother them. If you know how to properly remediate and fix the mold issue often times it will not be as expensive as people think.

I mentioned briefly one investor group I worked with preferred moldy houses and would send me in to the most grimy places because they knew that the majority of the time it was not that costly to fix the mold issue. Remember, if you are selling the off market deal to a first time homebuyer or novice investor mold will most likely scare them away so only sell those types of houses to the experienced guys.

Should You Work With Family And Friends?

One of the most often debated subject in real estate and business is the age old question of "Should you work with friends and family?" From my experience in real estate I have seen some partnerships with friends and family work out extremely well, while just as many have turned out horribly. It all depends on the people and the situation. My recommendation would be that if you do decide to work with friends and family make sure you know what you are doing in terms of the business. I would not start a partnership for your first deal, rather I recommend doing 10 deals and learning what can go wrong before starting any type of partnership because one little mistake could totally ruin a relationship. I would also advise that if you are working with friends and family maybe not necessarily doing so in a partnership.

For example, maybe once you have a steady business going you could see if your friends or family want to be lenders on any of your deals. Or maybe some of your friends or family are great with graphic design, writing, or any number of things and they can work with on a project-by-project basis and are not tied to the business 100%. Either way I would be very careful about this and only work with friends and family after gaining some experience in the real estate business. It is one of those things that sounds great on paper but can turn sour quickly.

I know of one example where a broker hired a friend as a favor who had been out of work and could not find any job anywhere for over a year. This should have been a red flag, you almost never want to hire anyone that can't find work somewhere else especially in a great economy, and the same is true with contractors. You only want to hire "busy" contractors because that means people like working with them. There is usually a good reason why someone has been unemployed for over a year in a strong job market and not surprisingly this person lasted about six months before the relationship grew too toxic. Not all of your friends or family are going to have the same goals and motivation as you, so that is why I would recommend working with them on a project-by-project basis.

Are Tenants A Deal Killer?

Sometimes you will come across real estate deals that have a ton of potential, however the house has tenants in them. Here is my advice on those types of deals. To begin with you should have a very good understanding of landlord and tenant laws in your jurisdiction. I have dealt with tenants in three different states around my metropolitan area and regulations are vastly different so make sure you do your research. In some states the process of removing tenants can take as little as 30 days, while in other states you can have what we call "professional tenants" who know how to work the system and can go over a year without paying and still not be evicted.

The next step is to evaluate your exit strategy, some investors, depending on the state and the situation would actually prefer that there are paying tenants in the property, while others want nothing to do with them. I had one house that I was selling to a rehabber and the seller told me the tenants would not be leaving until 21 days after closing. Three weeks! It was a great deal though, so what I did was I put my assignment fee of $10,000 into an escrow account after closing and I told my rehabber that for every day after that the seller did not leave I would pay them $100 from the escrow account.

This would keep me motivated to keep up my side of the deal and get the tenants out of there and also protect my rehabber at the same time. The deal worked out great and everybody was happy. I've also brought a buyer for cash flowing rental properties where my buyer did not even need to see the property since he knew the numbers in that particular area. All he wanted was a copy of the lease to verify the numbers and his end goal was to keep these tenants in place for as long as possible.

I've also had situations where I had to evict the tenant for non-payment and although it does not happen very often you will come across this situation and that is why you need to become an expert in your state's landlord and tenant laws. In some cases you will have a seller call you saying that they want to sell the property and that you will need to evict the tenant. For those you just have to plan for the worse case scenario and budget an extra five or ten thousand more to remove them.

One strategy that I have seen work with foreclosures and other types of properties is called cash for keys. In this situation you factor in basically "incentivizing" (read: bribing) the tenant to leave. You give them a couple of thousand dollars to move out and the property is yours. Again, each state is different and you should read as much as you can and always consult a real estate lawyer before buying one of these types of houses or employing any of the aforementioned strategies.

Stealing Deals

People ask me all the time in the off market business, what if one of your competitors tries to "steal" your deal? When I first got started in this business I used to think everyone was out to steal my deals. I had what you could call a scarcity mindset. Anytime I got a deal under contract I would go to the courthouse and actually file memorandum of contract paperwork to make sure that nobody else could steal it out from under me. I learned that doing that was a fairly extreme measure and almost not even worth my time. My friend even told me I had trust issues (among others) for doing that.

A person stealing your deal very rarely happens and it usually happens because of your own error not theirs. For example, if you have a property under contract do not put that house on Craigslist or you risk having all types of degenerates out there trying to take your deal. Or, do not work with shady people. I had a builder that I never worked with before who stole one of my deals. The seller was a difficult person to begin with which made things harder, but the bottom line make sure you have control of a property before telling anybody about it, unless you trust them 100%. The people who steal deals from you are not common and they typically do not last in this business because much of it is based on reputation.

All of the big investors I know, the guys doing 20, 30, 50+ houses a year are typically great to work with and will not do anything shady. You can't become the top house buyer doing shady things, so I would more worry about the smaller guys when it comes to getting a deal stolen. The bottom line is make sure you either have the property under contract before letting your buyers know and in the very rare instance that someone does steal your deal use it as a learning experience to make you a better and savvier investor.

Additional Red Flags

Some additional red flags I need to mention when doing business in the off market world are below.

The biggest one I would say is "weird houses." Now I know that sounds basic, but essentially I mean houses that are unlike the other houses in the neighborhood and not in a good way. Maybe every house in the neighborhood is a two-level 2000 square foot house and the property you are considering buying is a one-level 750 square foot house with two bedrooms and one bath.

I know this is an extreme example, but the point I am trying to make is that you need to have at least three comps of the same type of house. If the house you are looking to buy or sell is unusually different from the other houses you need to be very conservative. Another example I have seen is if the house is in front of a gas station or other unattractive type of commercial building like a power plant. You will need to lower your after renovated value in this case since (shocker) most people do not like living right next to a gas station, power plant, or highway.

Another issue I have seen pop up with off market deals is also related to comps. If you are the investor on the deal sometimes real estate agents or wholesalers will bring you amazing off market deals that on paper look like the deal of the century. What you need to watch out for is that sometimes they might unknowingly use comps from a different neighborhood or use comps that are not exactly what the property they are selling is.

Or sometimes the property they bring is so low priced compared to the general market, but there might not be any sold comps of this type of home. You need to see sold comps before pulling the trigger on any type of deal. I have seen condos in my area as low as 40K which I thought was the deal of the century...until I actually found comps from three years ago where the same condos sold for 20K and there has not been any sales since.

A third common issue to watch out for is you will get offered an off market deal and you might think it is from the owner but it isn't. A lot of times it will be a wholesaler calling you about the deal as if they are the actual seller. To take it a step further they might even be a wholesaler, wholesaling someone else's deal almost like a daisy chain of real estate.

To prevent this type of transaction all you have to do is ask the person that contacts you if they are the owner and you will quickly find out if they own the property or are wholesaling it or selling it. Keep in mind it is not necessarily a bad thing to buy from a wholesaler, but you should be in the know as to who you are actually buying the property from.

The Steroid Era Of Statistics

Ladies and Gentlemen we have entered what I like to call the "steroid era of stats". One of the most common things I would recommend looking out for in the real estate world (and in life) are how easily stats are manipulated these days. This section of the book applies to off market deals as well as to the real estate business in general and life as a whole. When I was in college I took a class called Statistics 101. One thing I learned in this class was how nearly any statistic can be made up or exaggerated and displayed to the point where it looks completely different than the actual truth behind the matter. Statistics can lie! This is especially true in the real estate field and I will give you several examples.

For starters, the most common "stat" you will see manipulated or incorrect are the after renovated values or repair values of properties that other investors and real estate agents send you. Many times another investor or real estate agent will unknowingly (or sometimes knowingly) send you inflated comps from a different neighborhood. Any comparable sales you look at should be essentially the same house and you should ideally have at least three recent sales from which to base your number on. That goes for rentals too, you should have at least three recent rentals to help you decide on the rental pricing of your property. It is also common for other investors or agents to greatly underestimate the cost of repairs involved in fixing up the home. Again you should run your own numbers.

In the next couple paragraphs I am going to pick on a local real estate agent I know (who I will keep anonymous), but whose stats are manipulated and misrepresented so much that he should win an award for it. You will see how easily people can be tricked into believing stats or claims and I will give just a couple of his own examples as well as how easily I could falsify my own stats.

Before I jump into that there was an amazing Instagram post by **@thebrokeagent** (please follow him) who summed up this trend of manipulating stats perfectly. He wrote "Real estate agents in Instagram are like this: entrepreneur, investor, builder, stager, point guard for the Knicks, broker, real estate agent, home flipper, speaker, coach, blogger, related to JFK, industry influencer, mother, father, agent, real estate soothsayer, co-host of the 'I sell nothing ever podcast,' on the board of neighborhood association of random city in California, top 3% of real estate agents a mile East of Tampa, loving cousin, President and CEO of a company that literally does nothing, astronaut, expert at things, Little League first base coach sometimes when it's convenient, motivational guru."

I hate to pick on this one real estate agent but his stats are so wildly manipulated, while at the same time he goes out of his way to claim that he is the honest real estate agent that I had to bring it up.

FSBOs and The Million Dollar Agent

The best example I can give was when I was first getting with his firm he told me to list as many For Sale By Owners properties as I could for free so that the next year I could tell potential clients I sold $50M worth of real estate. Now, doing an MLS placement free listing where all calls are directed to the seller requires a license and no skills, whereas actually selling $50M worth of real estate requires a ton of knowledge, dedication, and is completely different. If a seller or buyer did not know any better you could see how they could be easily manipulated by telling them I sold 50M or 100M.

This agent even won an award for selling $100M or something like that during his first year and bragged about it as if he actually did a full service listing for all these properties. I am almost certain that the real estate agent organization who gave him this award had no knowledge that this was an MLS placement service and not an actual listing. All he did was put the homes on the MLS for free and had the phone number go directly to the seller so that he didn't have to do any work outside of putting it on MLS. He did this to boost his numbers but portrayed it as if he was the top agent with these unbelievable numbers.

Facebook Groups

Or take another interesting example with a Facebook group that he started to try to bring more attention to off market properties. At the time, and possibly still to this day, there is a glitch in some Facebook business groups which allows you to add any of your friends to a group you start without getting their approval. You can see where this is going and you have probably been added to other Facebook groups without your knowledge or approval.

He reached out to as many real estate people as possible to have them shoot out this invite that automatically added people to the group. In return he could say he had 10,000 or so users in his group. In reality, probably 95% of these people had no idea they were even in that group. He actually approached someone about selling this group giving the potential investor the impression that these 10,000 or so agents had been built organically over time and not with some Facebook glitch that can rapidly add thousands of people. So again, he inflated his numbers dramatically and if you did not know any better you would think having 10,000 people in a group is very substantial and impressive.

Elon Musk?

Another interesting stat or claim he makes is that he is an angel investor in several startups. Now doesn't that make you think of some billionaire or millionaire funding people out in Silicon Valley? The truth of the matter is he puts money into Kickstarter campaigns which anybody can do with $20 and a user account with them. It is similar to me saying I was a co-owner in Nike. I owned some shares of the company, so technically speaking I was a co-owner and investor in Nike, but that's not something I brag about because that would be preposterous and completely misrepresented.

Off Market Vs FSBO

I know we have talked about the difference between off market homes and FSBO but just to reinforce this point with the made up stats, there is a huge difference between the two types of homes. This same agent now claims to be the "off market specialist with 2,000 homes a month" according to one of his profiles. However if we were to make him support those claims I doubt he could provide any evidence of any off market deals that he or his agents have done. What he is doing is just adding freely available For Sale By Owner listings to his search and then technically calling them "off market" to make it sound as if he digging up all these incredible deals. While I think that adding those listings is actually a good thing, it is just the way it is represented, along with all of his other stats that make me cringe.

Zillow Reviews

His Zillow profile is interesting as well and is another example of how stats can be manipulated. Zillow, if you are not aware, is a site where you can give reviews to agents based on their service, etc. They review agents based on as scale of five stars for if you bought or sold a house. However, there is a little known part of Zillow that allows you to get reviews even if you did not sell or buy a house.

Since you can tell this agent is good at using stats to his advantage you can see where this is going. About half of his five star reviews are from people that never bought or sold a property from him or any of his agents, although to people that don't know any better you would think these were all thrilled clients from past sales. He probably has more 5 star reviews from people that have never even done business with him than most agents have from actual real sales. I would be shocked if you could find any other agent manipulating stats like that on Zillow or elsewhere.

Shady Agents And Bullshit Artists

It is funny and ironic because like I mentioned this same real estate agent goes out of his way on his blog and elsewhere to let it be known that he is the "honest" real estate agent and to watch out for the real estate agents that make up shady stats just to make a commission. You now can see one reason why the real estate industry sometimes gets a bad name. It is very easy to manipulate data or words to boost your credentials. The bottom line with this agent is that all of his claims are actually partially true however the way they are represented is completely exaggerated. I think this agent has a part time job writing those incredulous Yahoo news headlines that you click on and then realize that there is only a kernel of truth from what the headline said.

I Am An Actor, Pro Basketball Coach, and International Philanthropist

Here are a couple examples of my own personal career and how I could change my "biography" or resume if I wanted to since all of these are technically true. I come from a basketball background and even got paid to coach a team one summer which technically speaking would make me a professional basketball coach. Additionally I have a bit role "acting" in a local award winning film and even got an IMDB (www.IMDB.com) credit for it. So I could say I am a professional actor as well. There is also an awesome charity that I have donated to in the past called Charity Water which provides clean drinking water to people in developing countries. Does that make me an international philanthropist if I donate $50?

If I wanted to update my credentials I could say that I am a former pro basketball coach, actor, and international philanthropist and all of this would be technically true however it would be completely misrepresented at the same time. I would recommend checking out the book by Ryan Holliday "Trust Me I'm Lying" which goes more in-depth into how stats, claims, and other things you thought to be true are often lies or just a kernel of truth in them.

Story

One of the first couple of deals I did I had two buyers that were very interested in my deal. One of them offered me $10,000 for the house and the other offered $17,000. I ended up going with the lower offer for a couple reasons. The people that made me the offer was a local couple that I knew was very active in the real estate investment community, they had other houses going on nearby and I knew they were going to close. The other guy that made me an offer for 17K I could not find online, I wasn't sure if he had ever bought any fixer uppers and the percentage of the deal closing with this guy was much slimmer.

I would prefer to go with the experts and make a smaller amount then go with a shady investor who might not be able to close. I can't tell you how many times I have heard of investors who a week before closing tell their agent or wholesaler that they can't close the deal, which is a disaster. To mitigate this risk you need to work with qualified people.

Conclusion

This chapter covers the most common mistakes I see all the time in the real estate off market industry. You should be well versed in all of them and I would invite you to do even more research on the topics we covered so you can be prepared when you find yourself in these types of situations. The great thing about real estate is that every deal you do builds confidence, makes me savvier, and I become less prone to aforementioned common mistakes. I look back on myself having done only five deals, then 10, then 20, etc and I see myself changing for the better, getting wiser with each deal made.

Action item

Start practicing with your deal analyzer on the website www.homevisor.com and start asking investors and contractors about how much they are paying to renovate. The goal is to get good at estimating, you don't necessarily need to know how something is going to be renovated more so just how much it might cost. Don't be afraid to ask other investors as Meetup groups or even watching some of the popular house flipping shows you can get a general idea of what items cost.

Also, if you have liked what you read so far I invite you to take the next step to get additional resources on the off market world including cool training videos, updates, live coaching, and more. All you have to do is text **OFFMARKET to 444999** to stay updated on everything going on in the off market world.

CHAPTER 6

Building Your Off Market Team

Building a team of real estate professionals is one of the most important parts of this business. We are going to cover the full spectrum of how to build a team similar to the 1994 Dream Team of USA basketball that won a Gold Medal at the Olympics and is widely recognized as the greatest and most talented team of all time. When I first got started in off market deals I did not fully understand this and I would just go with the first title company, first real estate agent, first hard moneylender, and first wholesaler that responded, until I understood the concept of casting a wide net and then cherry picking.

Cherry Picking Theory

The first strategy I have to tell you about is what I like to call the cherry picking theory. This applies to the leads you will be getting in your business as well as when it comes to building your team. Keep in mind you are looking for that rare (one in

10) real estate professional who is active in the real estate investment industry or off market business, specializes in working with investors, and seems like a good person to work with. As you begin your real estate journey you will find many real estate professionals have no desire whatsoever to be in the real estate investment industry, while others are in it full-time.

When it comes to the Cherry Picking Theory this applies not just to your investor friendly real estate agent, this applies to investor friendly agents, title companies, contractors, and more. You should not be trying to convince anyone to be investor friendly, rather you should be looking for the "low hanging fruit" that is readily available and already making off market deals. One of the best ways to build your team is to ask established off market specialists or investors or agents for the best title companies, lenders, contractors, and more. Typically they will not have an issue with providing names since they may even get referral money in some instances. Do your research, attend real estate networking events, talk to as many real estate professionals as you can, and you will start to grow your dream team.

Building A Team Of Real Estate Agents

Real estate agents can be a valuable source of off market leads for your business. Even though most real estate agents will list properties on the MLS there will be many who will potentially give you first access to any fixer uppers they have coming on the market. The best way to find investor friendly real estate agents is making a list of real estate agents who have sold properties for investors in the past.

You can then reach out to these people and stay in touch with them letting them know that if they do come across any fixer upper deals to allow you the opportunity to make an offer on them and letting them keep the full six percent commission and/or giving the standard three percent back to the seller. You will need to reach out to a lot of real estate agents to find the ones that are friendly, competent, AND active in the investment industry.

I had a friend who worked for a very successful investor and one of his main strategies was networking with agents. He compiled a list of all the agents who had done a deal in the last six months and proceeded to contact them all via phone, text, and email, letting them know he was an investor and he was looking for deals. He also let the agents know they could be the listing agent if they found him any good deals. Out of the 1,000 or so agents on the list about 50 began to send him deals and he always had a steady flow of properties.

Find The Right Title Company

It is very important to find investor friendly title companies who can work with assignment fees, fast closings, and are equipped to handle tough liens and other issues that can arise from distressed properties. The best way to find a great investor friendly title company is through referrals from other active investors, hard money lenders, and/or investor friendly real estate agents.

Don't be afraid to ask other fellow investors, this is one resource that most professionals will not care about referring; sometimes they might even get a referral fee from the title company itself. You can certainly cold call a list of title companies like I did when I first got started, however I'm not sure it's the most effective strategy. Ideally you want to build a list of about five title companies that do a lot of work with investors.

The downside of working with a traditional title company is that they are used to seeing the same type of conventional financing 30-45 day close and they might be caught off guard with other types of transactions. Try to find three investor-friendly title companies that you get referred to from other investors and use them all to see which one is better. Some title companies are a big operation with a large staff and a professional office while others might be a one or two person shop in a strip mall or one room in a building. The only thing that matters is if they do a good job or not so I would recommend trying all of the ones that come recommended.

Hard Money Lenders Are Everything

Hard money lenders are another group of professionals that can be a great asset. This is an interesting topic because with hard moneylenders you will find such a wide range of professionals. Some hard moneylenders will be the nicest people you have ever talked to, while others not so much. Most old school hard moneylenders have a reputation of being a little on the arrogant side to say the least, however it is not hard to find the easy to work with lenders. All you have to do is call them and within five minutes you can get a great idea of how they operate.

There are some amazing hard moneylenders that have free trainings on their website, deal analyzers on their site, and some that will even partner with you on deals if you are not comfortable doing a large rehab. Hard moneylenders typically have the best buyers lists as well so if you have a sweet deal that you are not sure about you can ask them and they might have a buyer for you.

Hard moneylenders can be found through Google, LinkedIn, as well as referrals from other investors. Eventually you will start to hear the same names over and over again and chances are those are the best people to work with. You will also find through your networking that other investors including your experienced competitors might be willing to offer hard money loan to you on a deal by deal basis, sometimes at a lower rate than the Hard Money lenders, so keep that in mind as well. Once you get established as a real estate professional, you can even start lending hard money on local deals since after a couple years you will have a good understanding of the business.

Wholesaling Team

Wholesalers will be an important part of your team and to be successful you should keep a database of all the active wholesalers in your area. Just like many other systems there will be the 80/20 rule. 20 percent of the wholesalers will have 80 percent of the deals so it's key that you find the most active ones.

What you want to do is stay in touch with these wholesalers once a month or so to see what deals they are working on. They will send you a lot of bad off market deals, however they will also send you a lot of great deals (if you have a lot of them) and it's your job to not only train them on what you are looking for, but also respond quickly if you do come across a good deal. I would say on average about one in 10 properties they send to me are deals I would actually consider. However, every now and then they come across Grand Slam type of deals so they are definitely an important part of any team. When you combine working with wholesalers and real estate agents and you have a direct marketing system like direct mail in place you will start to see a lot of deal opportunities.

Do You Need A Real Estate Mentor Or Coach?

Real estate mentors and coaches is one of the most controversial parts of the real estate industry. There are many coaching programs out there and many people that think they don't need coaching. Here is my take on coaching: you need a coach! The only reason you wouldn't need a coach or mentor is that you don't care about being more successful. It's amazing to me how small minded and arrogant some investors, real estate agents, and others can be when it comes to coaching.

They think they are above it. Usually it's some real estate professional that is doing pretty well, making six figures who thinks they don't need coaching. What they don't realize is that there are people making 10 and 20 times what they make that still seek out coaches. Many of the Fortune 500 CEOs who are making millions of dollars a year have coaches among other successful people. To me it is kind of hilarious because Michael Jordan had a shooting coach, Tiger Woods has a swing coach, and there are some local real estate professionals that think they are above having a coach.

The purpose of a coach is to give you a different perspective and help you tweak things here and there to reach your potential. The coach does not even necessarily have to be more successful than you; they just have to be competent, motivated, and full of ideas. It could be one idea they give you that leads to another idea that gives you an idea that can add more profit, more time, or something else to your business. Personally I have paid quite a large sum for coaching and the reason is this: if you pay for something you are going to value it so much more.

Of course there is tons of free information out there, but I have found when I pay for something, especially something expensive I tend to take way more action. In fact, I stayed up late at night thinking of how much I had just paid for a coaching program, had told some people about it who thought I was crazy. This led to massive action taking and internalizing every tidbit of the information. To be successful you need as many new ideas coming into your possession as possible because you never know what idea is going to take you to the next level.

In my business I am looking for every possible advantage to beat my competition. I have paid coaches as well as "free ones." Some great places to get "coached" for free are YouTube videos of interviews of real estate professionals, books, courses, and more.

Mastermind Your Way To Success

Mastermind groups are a great way to take your business to the next level and find more off market deals. These are usually held once a quarter and bring together successful people in any industry. Usually these cost money to join, however if you have ever read Napoleon Hill's Think and Grow Rich you know how valuable these can be. One of the most famous mastermind groups out there currently is Joe Polish's 25K group where successful entrepreneurs pay $25,000 a year to join. Look it up on YouTube.

They have some great interviews from people in all different industries. There are also many real estate investing mastermind groups out there, look up the Collective Genius. You need to realize for a mastermind group to succeed they can only accept the cream of the crop and I know to qualify for Collective Genius you have to be doing somewhere around 100 deals a year just to be considered. I know some people that will just invite random people to a Ruby Tuesday and call it a "Mastermind" group. That is not a mastermind group. The whole point of a mastermind is that it is the cream of the crop.

What happens at a Mastermind group is that you go over what is working in your business, what you need help with, and a group of other successful peers can give you ideas to help your business, let you know what's working for them and more. I am in a mastermind group with many high achievers, most of whom are on a higher level of business than me which in turn motivates me to step up. Another benefit of being in one is knowing that every quarter or every six months you know that you will have to talk about what's going on in your business so that motivates you to be in friendly, healthy competition with the other people in the group and step your game up.

Usually mastermind groups are held in exotic locations or fun cities where you get to know other participants on a social level as well. When you are working all the time this can be a great way to change up your routine and get you more energized with great ideas to implement when you get back home.

Finding The Right Contractor

Finding good contractors can be one of the most difficult and frustrating things to do. But, lucky for you, you've got a copy of this book so you will know how to find the best ones. Every major city or even a small town has real estate agents that work there (shocker I know). All you have to do is Google "real estate agent (insert your city here)" and you will typically find 20, 30, or even 50 real estate agents that come up. Go to their website and almost always they will have a "vendor list" of recommended contractors.

Find five to 10 agents and build up a huge vendor list then you can cross reference some of these contractors on Yelp or

Angie's List. Then, if you are working on a project invite three of them to give you a bid and go with the best most professional contractor that you get along with.

Additional People You Will Need

Additional people that you will need for your real estate business include CPAs, mortgage brokers, and insurance Agents. These are all people you want referrals from. None of these people you should hire unless you read they have amazing yelp reviews (seriously). You need a great CPA and the best way is to ask other real estate professionals whom they use as well as doing some online research. Mortgage brokers and insurance agents are another key part of your team who you can usually find through referrals from other professionals in your field

Story

An interesting place to find great ideas and get ideas on how to build your dream team is real estate podcasts and YouTube interviews. There are plenty of those out there where they interview different investors and off market specialists who go over what is currently working in their location. After listening to these podcasts you typically are so full of ideas and open-minded to what is possible.

    My advice with these podcasts and interviews is to choose one thing from the 30-minute or hour-long interview and implement it. If you implemented one thing from every podcast you would be a testing machine and I can almost guarantee your success. What I have found from my own marketing experiments is when I try different things, usually one in three or one in five work out the way it was planned, the others flop. Even with those that don't work out I gain valuable experience.

The faster you experiment the faster you can see what really works. There is nothing like testing a marketing experiment and hitting it out of the park.

Conclusion

With building your dream team for off market real estate deals you want to cast your net wide so that you can find the 10% or so of real estate professionals who work in the investment industry and understand what types of deals you are looking for. In my business I have specialists for everything. I don't just use the generic Title Company or basic real estate agent down the street that you meet at the County Fair. Everyone on my team is an expert and if I get a lead or some issue that needs further research I will reach out to the expert in that area.

There are people in every industry that specialize in something and if they don't specialize in one niche they are missing out on a lot of business. Major Key: if you want to make more and do more deals, you should be known as something i.e. the condo expert, the off market expert, the tax lien expert. People will flock to you.

Action item

Start building your dream team roster with a simple Excel spreadsheet. You should start building a list of names under Real estate agents, Hard Moneylenders, Title Companies, Contractors, and more. Under each category there should be at least five different people or companies and then from that initial five there should be one or two that seem better than others. Online research and networking are the best places to start and just be consistent adding a couple names every week. Over time, as you add to this list you can qualify the roster even more and find the best of the best for each position.

Also, if you have liked what you read so far I invite you to take the next step to get additional resources on the off market world including cool training videos, updates, live coaching, and more. All you have to do is text **OFFMARKET to 444999** to stay updated on everything going on in the off market world.

CHAPTER 7

The Major Keys To Off Market Success

In this chapter we are going to be covering the major keys to off market success. I will go into specifics so you know exactly the blueprint myself and other investors use to consistently find highly discounted off market deals.

Massive Action Always Wins

Take massive action! One of the main strategies of the top off market dealmakers is taking massive action. I know that phrase sounds like something you hear in any motivational or strategic book, but I will tell you exactly what I mean by that. When I was getting started I would send out 20-30 letters a week to sellers of inherited properties and I would get some calls here and there and typically they were actually good leads, but there weren't too many of them. Since I am always seeking the best way of doing real estate investing I paid for a consulting session with one of the top off market investors in the US. It was not cheap and it lasted just 30 minutes, but what I learned on that call shook my worldview to its core.

My main issue was not getting consistent leads and I wanted to know how to fix that situation. I basically picked his brain for 30 minutes and even tried to keep him on the phone longer after learning some of his strategies. He told me his best strategy was sending out 10,000 postcards PER MONTH to absentee owners. Usually with postcards your response rate is anywhere from 1-3% and he was getting literally hundreds of leads each and every month and just cherry picking the best ones. He actually had an acquisitions assistant who would coordinate to have his mailers sent out and then the assistant would also filter the leads and only show my investor friend the best of the best that he would then put under contract. Here I was in my market sending out a couple hundred letters a week or month and this guy was sending out 10,000 each month. I was not taking massive action.

I was taking action, but not enough to have any level of consistency with my deal flow or achieve the results I wanted. What you will realize in this business is that leads are the lifeblood of the off market business. No leads means no deals. With all of your marketing you need to think scalability and massive action.

There is a marketing legend named Gary Halbert who I suggest people read up on. He was famous for taking so much action when he was getting started with direct mail that he was spending all his money on direct mail and literally did not have enough to pay his electric bill and therefore did not have any electricity at home. He eventually made millions and his advice on direct mail and marketing is priceless. I would recommend getting his book The Boron Letters, or really any book by him.

In regards to bandit signs, I actually don't do bandit signs, but if I did I would make sure that I put up 100 each and every month, at a minimum. Putting up 25 bandit signs each and every week is not terribly difficult, especially since you can most likely outsource that task to a local kid looking for work. As far as your budget for marketing with off market deals you should start small, I started with about $50 a week, however as soon as I made my first deal I scaled it up. You certainly do not need to spend this much, but one of the top investors I know in the country spends close to 100K (not 10K) each and every month. That is what I would call taking massive action!

Modeling Successful People

Model the right people: In this business you find that every single person has an opinion on what you should do or not do to find great real estate deals. The world is much the same way: broke people will give you advice on money, divorced people will give you advice on relationships, jobless people giving advice on finding jobs, and the list goes on and on. It is amazing how many completely unqualified people will give you advice on things they have no business giving advice on.

For example, this one agent in my area could give you every reason why you should not invest in real estate, yet he has never completed a successful investment real estate deal. The only people you should listen to are people at the top of their game in real estate with a focus on investment and off market properties. They are harder to find but definitely out there. Look for coaches and coaching programs that offer a lot of value where you can see testimonials of everyday people doing off market real estate transactions.

Or if you do not want to spend money on coaching look up YouTube interviews on Biggerpockets and Flipnerd, in those interviews a lot of times the investors and off market specialists will tell you almost exactly what they are doing in their business to be successful. Never stop learning! I know some successful real estate agents as well as investors who are very good at real estate, but could be even better if they were more humble and coachable.

Many people in this business hit a certain level of income and think that they know it all and there is no way or reason to improve. Always realize that there are people out there crushing real estate so much more than you. Remember, if Michael Jordan had a shooting coach and Tiger Woods has a swing coach maybe you should have a real estate mentor. If you are too frugal to spend money on coaching at least read books on finding investment deals and make sure to implement the strategies talked about in there to see which ones are the best.

Measure For Improvement

Measure your business. Your business activity should be measured on at least a month-to-month basis if not a weekly basis. The famous saying goes "you can only improve what you measure" and this embodies the idea that evolving to the next level of real estate starts with measuring the actions and strategies you are using. Examples of some of the things to track when you are starting out in the real estate business could be as simple as how many leads are you generating per month.

That can be as easy as purchasing a small dry erase board and putting it on the end of your desk and noting your progress. You should also measure how much you spend on your business each month so that you can find out your lead cost. When I got started a coach had told me that 50 leads should equal a deal. As a result, I made it my goal to get 10 additional leads every single month until I was consistently generating 50 leads per month. When you hit that magical number you will see great opportunities for yourself or for your investors.

You should also measure other variables like how much profit you make on the average deal if you are doing a transaction as a buyer's agent, wholesaler, or rehabber. If you want to learn more about this type of tracking I suggest looking into KPI metrics. Many people don't do this or are not familiar with this simple strategy, and in time it can help you operate on a level above your competition.

Persistence And Resilience

One of the best qualities for success I have noticed in the real estate business is being persistent. What I mean by this is when you start to do your marketing you may think that you are going to have 100 leads by tomorrow. Usually that is not the case and you are in for a harsh reality check. I remember when I first got started with marketing I put up 20 bandit signs and got a separate phone to answer all the calls I thought I was going to get.

That didn't happen immediately. The reality is that sometimes your phone will ring off the hook unexpectedly, while other times you might send out 500 postcards and only get a call or two. Don't let this discourage you, because you are still taking action. One of the best parts of the real estate business is learning how to market because these marketing skills are transferable to most any business. I get offers all the time from people wanting me to teach them how to market because I am able to use so many different channels of marketing very effectively (direct mail, pay per click, SEO, YouTube, and others).

I sometimes find it helpful to remind myself that I am in the marketing business not necessarily the real estate business. This paradigm shift has helped me to be successful in this business, and I am willing to bet it will help you, too. It's funny because there are people out there with highly advanced real estate degrees from prestigious colleges, but if they don't how to make the phone ring it won't matter. I may not have those degrees, but I have valuable, real world experience that creates my consistent lead flow, which will beat them every time.

If you are just starting out, the ideal situation is that six months to a year from now you want to be an expert in at least three forms of marketing. For me, I got very good at first direct mail, then I learned pay per click, and at this writing am growing my command of YouTube. I am constantly looking to add more tools to my marketing toolbox, and you should be too! Sharpening your marketing skills always pays off and you would be shocked at how much free information is available online to help you utilize these various forms of lead generation.

Referring Your Way To Success

The fifth key to off market success is building the right team around you, which we touched on earlier, and the best way to do that is through referrals. When you are at networking events for real estate always keep your eyes and ears open for the best of the best in terms of title companies, contractors, investors, agents, and more. It is much easier than you think for a bad investor or bad real estate agent or even bad title company to screw your deal up and leave you without a profit. LinkedIn is another great place to start building your team.

On that site you can sort people in your area by the real estate investment industry. I would suggest starting to build your team immediately. You can organize your different experts with a CRM (Customer Relationship Management) tool or simply use an Excel spreadsheet like I did when I first got started. You should continually be looking for new talent to add to your team. I remember I thought I had a pretty good team when I first got started but I had only met a small percentage of the people in the local real estate industry. I was not yet aware how many people are in the real estate business. You need to make sure you are finding the investment specialist or off market specialist.

How To Learn Your Neighborhood

The best ways to learn your neighborhood which will help you in the off market business as well as just in general are rather obvious but worth talking about. The first strategy is touring the neighborhood. Now there are a couple things I would recommend with this. One interesting thing to do is look up the celebrity houses in your area. Most cities will have compiled some sort of list of famous people in your area. This can be a great and interesting way to spend a few hours, and as an added bonus (if you're into that kind of thing) you could possibly spot a celebrity. I even once drove to a Presidential candidate's house only to be met by black SUVs and bodyguards.

Another thing I did quite a bit when I was starting out was driving out to the house of any lead that I got. So, even if it was a "bad" lead or unmotivated seller I would still drive the street, check out the area and gain a new level of comfort with it in case I came across another lead there in the future. You should also be reading as much as you can about any neighborhood where you might be buying properties.

You want to know about any new developments, what the buzz is in that part of town, what store just opened up, etc. Anytime I am out an appointment in a part of town I have never been to I try to check out a local café or restaurant and get a feel and vibe for the neighborhood. Between actually driving around the streets, reading about them online, and even looking at Google Earth, within a couple months you should have a solid understanding of your target market area(s). Some investors I know even know every house on the block on certain streets and some even know most of the people that live there too, almost as if they would be running for a local political office.

CRM (Customer Relationship Manager)

If you want to take your business to the next level you need a CRM also known as a Customer Relationship Manager. When I first got started in this business, my CRM was a basic Microsoft Excel spreadsheet. This worked for a little while, but as my business was growing it started to drive me crazy. Outgrowing my starter tools was a good sign! Once you implement what you're learning in this book and your business begins to grow you will need a true CRM, too.

They are not that expensive, in fact there are many options ranging from free to the expensive variety with more advanced features. A CRM system organizes your leads and contacts and you can even sort them by value or by customer potential. Another thing a CRM enables you to do is keep track of your interaction with the prospect and make important notes about the deal. Every note you input is saved into the system, which will allow you to be prepared every time you talk with them. Perhaps the best feature of these CRMS is the calendar and reminder functions of when to contact or follow up with prospects. All you have to do is set a date and input whether you need to call, email, or text and the CRM will remind you of it. Most businesses will contact a prospect once.

You can gain a huge advantage by being persistent, and automatic reminders are a useful tool. Since there are so many CRMs widely available I would use one of the established ones. I had an old broker who never had heard of a CRM and instead of using any one of the hundreds of widely available ones he decided he was going to build his own. The result was a spreadsheet with confusing formulas spread out across the pages. I would advise against reinventing the wheel. Make use of the tools that are readily available, especially since there are so many widely available free options. My recommendation would be to read online reviews, maybe even try a couple, and implement one. It will be one of the best decisions you will make.

Vacation Time

Taking a vacation can sometimes be a "tough" thing but is actually going to be a huge part of your success. When you are focused on finding deals and business is humming along you might not want to take a vacation, but we all need a break every now and then. For the sake of your mental and physical health as well as your overall creativity and productivity, you must take a vacation! Time off can give you a new perspective, decreases your chances of burnout, and typically boosts your energy level.

Leonardo Da Vinci has a famous quote where he said, "every now and then go away, have a little relaxation, for when you come back to your work your judgment will be surer. Go some distance away because then the work appears smaller and more of it can be it can be taken in at a glance and a lack of harmony and proportion is more readily seen." I have also noticed that for some reason any time I go on vacation I come back and there is a huge deal opportunity that it presents itself upon my return. I think I need to go to Mexico more often now that I think about it. I also find that I am very productive in the week leading up to my vacation due to the impending deadline.

With all the excitement building up over your vacation you typically wake up earlier, stay later, and make sure you completely crush it at work the week before vacation. Sometimes your best ideas can come when you are not thinking about work, when your mind is completely immersed in scuba diving or some other activity and boom all of sudden you get that million dollar idea! I'm almost at the point where I want to try an experiment of going on more vacations at regularly scheduled intervals to see how much more productive I can be during the week. I recommend trying to visit new and interesting places that can challenge, inspire, and rejuvenate you.

Being A Spy

I am from a major metropolitan area with lots of people from different countries and I can tell you there are spies everywhere, I mean like Russian spies and others and I want you to become a spy as well, not in any nefarious type of way so let me explain what I mean. No, I'm not paranoid there is probably an article every other month about one being caught or a story about some international plot that was uncovered. When I say you should become a spy this is what I mean: you should be "spying" (read: researching) on your competitors as well as other businesses that you like or dislike for that matter.

See what ads your competitors are placing online, look at their direct mail pieces. Dig deep and find out what they are doing that is working and what tools may be useful for your business. I am not advocating doing anything illegal or unethical here, but merely am raising a valuable point: everyone else is researching the competition and if you're not doing it, then you're falling behind.

Practice your spying skills by paying closer attention when you visit businesses that you frequent on a daily or weekly basis. Think about outstanding experiences you've had at recent local businesses as well as horrible experiences that you've had and why they were bad or good. There are no bad examples. There are good, good examples and good, bad examples. Try to learn from everyone and every situation you encounter. Depending on the customer experience, you should either try to implement that into your own real estate business or make sure you do the complete opposite. I love to learn from both good and bad examples, and you should too.

Branding Your Business

Branding yourself and your business is another important factor since many people will be looking up your name, company name, and contact information online. It is important that you have a basic understanding of online branding, including setting up at the very least a LinkedIn profile and company website. Some more advanced options are YouTube, Instagram, Twitter, and any of the other social media channels.

My recommendations for setting up a LinkedIn profile is to spend about 30 minutes or so reading articles online of how to set up a good profile. LinkedIn is free to use and a very helpful resource. The next thing I would do in creating your profile is to browse other real estate professionals for good examples. Then just model your profile after those. There is no need to re-invent the wheel.

To set up a company website there are countless real estate investor or real estate templates that you can use to set yours up. Or if you want to spend a couple hundred bucks or so you can hire graphic and/or web designers and offer guidance via a few sample websites that you want to model yours after. The other online branding like YouTube and social media I would start as a hobby to learn the different strategies. Once you master these marketing channels then I would make them a larger part of your business development.

Adding Services

Ok there is a theory of mine that I think every real estate entrepreneur should be doing. You should continually be adding to the menu of additional services you can offer to clients. What I mean by that is you might start out your real estate career as a rental agent. Then, after getting more experience you start doing buyer agent deals, and then add listings to your repertoire. Now you might feel comfortable enough to start buying off market or investment properties for yourself.

The idea is to keep adding systems in place where you don't necessarily need to be doing more work and you can outsource them. Some of the top real estate entrepreneurs I know have a real estate brokerage arm of their business, an investment arm (of off market deals), an education arm where they coach people on how to be successful in real estate, and then maybe some type of more speculative arm like new construction or commercial deals or hard money lending. I can guarantee you that you will make more money this way, have a more thorough understanding of your craft, and it will keep you from getting bored.

This last part is important because if I was doing the same stuff for 10, 20, 30 years that would drive me crazy. It keeps things fun and interesting to continually be adding profitable services. Here are a few things you could think about adding as services to your current business: 1) property management, 2) development (flips), 3) become an associate or principal broker, 4) coach newer investors and agents, 5) speak in public about real estate, 6) write a book or create a product on real estate, 7) start hard money lending on deals in your area, 8) buy a small apartment building (instead of single family rental).

Sketchy Houses and Situations

Occasionally you will visit some bad houses in rough neighborhoods when looking for off market deals and here is the best advice I can give you to stay safe and secure.

Vacant Homes With No Doors

Some houses that have been vacant for a while actually have people that sleep in various parts of the house, also known as drifters. If you see evidence of drifters like a sleeping area with food or supplies you need to be very careful. You probably should not go into that house by yourself.

I usually come back with a friend, ideally a large friend. I remember a house out in a wooded community where there was gang graffiti everywhere and the seller had basically just let the property go. There was not even a lock on the front door and the door was just open. I should have probably gone with someone, but I was new to the business and walked around the entire house making a video while holding a two-by-four in my hand in case anyone came out. I learned a lot from this experience and next time I made sure to bring someone with me.

Drifters and Stolen Pipes

I would be sure to not sneak up on anyone either. By that I mean you should knock on the door a couple times before entering in case it is vacant and if you hear anyone inside when they shouldn't be then don't enter. I have walked in on an active robbery, a naked person, ferocious pit bulls, and more. The first thing I usually do with a house I am not sure about is walk the perimeter to look for any broken windows, evidence of people living there, etc.

One time I had actually seen someone in the backyard kind of walking away from the direction of the house into an alley. That should have been somewhat of a red flag, however I still proceeded to go inside the house (after knocking several times) and after five or so minutes inside I glanced up towards the second level and actually saw a person there trying to be as still as possible but was most likely stealing the copper pipes.

In some states, such as Maryland, is actually very common for people to steal the copper pipes and the copper from the air conditioner condenser units. I immediately left the house and this house was listed with an agent so I called them letting them know their house was being robbed. The bottom line is you must be on your toes with these properties.

Tenants and Evictions

A third lesson is do not try to reason with angry tenants in person, use the sheriff instead. If they are being unreasonable, not paying, or whatever it may be, give them their warning and then call the sheriff in. The way the eviction process works in most states is you call the sheriff to present the tenant with an eviction notice. This is a common practice.

You do not want to be in a hostile situation with a deadbeat who has nothing to lose. I have had to evict people before and been present at several other evictions and trust me you want to have professionals there who are licensed to carry weapons for self-defense. Evictions or just the threat of eviction can lead to increased tensions with some people so that is why you want to use professionals. Keep in mind with off market deals, this type of stuff very rarely happens, but if you have been in the business long enough (non-exaggerated) statistics predict that you will eventually come across it so be prepared. You should be proactive as well and try to learn the eviction process in your area so that you have a better understanding of what is going on.

Security Devices

A bonus strategy I have seen investors use is video cameras as well as inexpensive security systems for the properties they might be working on. Nowadays, cameras are fairly inexpensive and you can set them up to stream live to your computer so that you can keep an eye on your property 24/7. My brother did that for the house he lived in since all of his packages from Amazon were getting stolen. Now he has a camera right above his door to catch whoever was doing this.

Some investors I know buy security systems that are motion sensors that you can place in the kitchen and living rooms so that if it detects anyone walking around it will start beeping loudly and also ring your phone. I worked for an investor who would get many calls like that where he would send me to check on a property after having been alerted. There are security systems than range from $50 up to thousands of dollars and I would recommend getting one if you are not sure about the area or house.

Next Level Stuff

Okay, let's talk about some next level stuff to make sure you have every advantage going for you. Your day-to-day and week-to-week business should be a productive and fast paced endeavor and to do that you need to be sure your mind and body are running optimally.

The first thing I would recommend is eating well, and by that I don't mean heavy steak dinners—unless of course you just did a major deal. What I mean is you should eat reasonably healthy foods that keep you alert and give you energy. I am not saying you should become a vegan, however you should do a little bit of looking into healthy foods and keep track of what makes you feel good and what makes you feel tired. One agent I worked with said that the advantage to working with him is that he offered "free lunch" everyday. What he actually meant was that he would make these vegan smoothies from a dirty blender and share half of them with anyone who was in the office. You don't need to be that extreme, but you should be healthy.

Working out is another major key that you should regularly, ideally at least five times a week. This can help pump more oxygen to the brain and just get you on a slightly elevated level. Join a class if you have to or just go solo but either way there have been countless studies done that say working out can make you more productive. A lot of the classes these days in major metropolitan areas are great places to meet people and just try something new.

Meditate. There are many entrepreneurs that say meditation is one of the most important things you can do in business. Meditation helps clear your mind and will give you laser like focus after you've had some practice. There are many different forms of meditation, but at its most basic level it is essentially deep breathing. If we want to take the mindfulness practice a step further I would recommend yoga and/or getting massages on a weekly or monthly basis. All of these "non-business" activities can help you decompress and lead to you functioning at a highly aware, relaxed, and focused level.

Sleep. Your sleep is one of the most important parts of your business and let me explain. The feeling you have after a wonderful night's sleep is one-of-a-kind. You feel like you can take on anything the next day. Whereas the feeling you have after only a few hours of sleep is miserable. You can't focus the next day and you feel unmotivated. Take extra care to get a good night sleep, put on white noise when you sleep, use blackout shades, splurge on a mattress, and do anything you can to ensure you are well rested. A friend of mine even recommended a natural herbal remedy for sleep called Melatonin which is amazing. I look for every little advantage possible, because why not?

Virtual Assistants and Outsourcing

In terms of leveraging your time I would recommend hiring virtual assistants before you make the jump to hiring any employees or independent contractors. Places like Upwork.com and Fiverr.com are great places to find inexpensive labor that can take a lot of tedious work off of your plate. Some examples of things they can do are building your buyers list of investors, researching properties for you to market to, editing any of your videos, designing marketing materials, and much more.

Chances are if you have any type of online work or repetitive work that you do on a regular basis then it can be outsourced. I have one person who works 25 hours a week for me online researching the best properties to market to and compiling a list that she sends to me once a week. The cost to me comes out to about five dollars an hour. I know some entrepreneurs who have built entire businesses around virtual assistants. If this intrigues you then I suggest you look up Eben Pagan.

The best way to hire a virtual assistant is to make sure they have good reviews and have done the type of project you are looking to do. Then the next step is hire two of them for the same project and see who does a better job. This is a great way of "top grading" and finding out who might be the better long-term prospect for you. You would be amazed how different the results can be between two different people for the exact same job. I would also advise using the free software Screenomatic to create virtual trainings for any assistant you bring on. Screenomatic captures your screen and you can upload the videos to YouTube which in turn you can train your assistant without having to spend a lot of time with them.

I typically like to make a quick five-minute video on a given topic, like "how to make an eviction list," and then I will send the video over to them along with some basic instructions. These tools help me to ensure I get the work done the way I need it done for my systems to work efficiently.

Checklists Will Save Your Life

If you want your off market business to have any amount of consistency and dependability you are going to need to create checklists for different parts of your business. They may seem tedious, but having a checklist can increase efficiency, eliminate mistakes, and take your business to the next level. When creating checklists you need to think of your business as the "prototype for 5,000 more just like it" as Michael Gerber states in the E-Myth. You want to pretend as if you are going to franchise your business so that you can create repeatable business systems.

Creating an amazing system gives anybody you hire a way of doing things with consistency and gives you the results you are looking for. I know some investors and agents who are all over the place with their business, one week getting a ton of leads while the next not getting any since they have no systems or checklists. The most profitable real estate companies typically have the best systems that are not dependent on any one person.

If that person were to leave they could still replace them since their system and checklists are in place. As a quick example, a system for marketing with a checklist would be obtaining a direct mail list and sending the target prospect five letters over the course of six months and having this entire process outsourced. Most agents or investors will send out mail sporadically if they even mail at all and they have no consistency whatsoever. I would highly recommend reading Michael Gerber's E-Myth. That book goes into more depth on the power of checklists to leverage your business and take it to the next level.

Recommended Vendors

Whether you are brokering an off market deal, buying it for yourself to rehab, wholesaling it, or keeping the property as a rental you should have a substantial resource list of vendors. As you start your real estate career you should keep your eyes and ears open for good contractors, good title companies, good vendors, really anything that can help you in the real estate industry. You can keep these people on a Google Drive document, Excel spreadsheet, or CRM but you need to keep track of these people.

You would be amazed that just by adding a recommended contractor here or there over the course of a year can really add to up creating basically a dream team of resources. If you are buying the house yourself, obviously you will need to have a list of recommended people to get the job done and fix the property. If you are an agent, probably one of the most frequently asked questions is, "do you know a good contractor for this?"

It is an added service and your clients will love you for it if you can give them a name and contact information for their project. It is even better if you can send them the entire vendor list that they can keep. Many brokerages will actually have an "all star" list of vendors they have used in the past for all different types of real estate services. This would be a great place to start if you don't have one. All you have to do is ask your brokerage for it. Keep in mind with this list that you should also be constantly updating. Sometimes contractors do a terrible job and you should remove them or other times you might find an amazing contractor who is not on the list. Always be building this list.

Should You Quit Your Day Job?

Once you start doing off market deals or real estate deals in general when is a good time to quit your day job? My suggestion is to have at least three off market deals under your belt before considering making that decision. I would even advise keeping a part-time job when getting started, which is what I did. Ideally you would want to have saved up at least six months or a year's worth of income to support yourself while you get your real estate career off the ground.

I would also advise getting some type of part-time real estate job that can complement your business. This part-time job can also teach you things about real estate that you may not know, in addition to providing a steady stream of income. The time when you should fully quit your job is when you are getting so many leads (100 per month) and doing enough deals (two per month) that you absolutely need to quit your job to focus on your new business.

I even know one investor that did 10 off market deals while keeping his full-time job and did not quit until he had completed that 10th deal. It all depends on the risk level you can tolerate. Everybody is different. Keep in mind that real estate is not like a nine to five job where you get a paycheck every two weeks. Some deals can take six months or even up to a year to close, so you will need to learn to budget for such occurrences.

Day To Day Schedule

What should your schedule look like as a real estate entrepreneur? Usually my days are scheduled like this. I wake up early 6am or 7am and grab a cup of coffee and immediately start working on the highest priority task, which is usually getting my marketing out (e.g. sending out my direct mail from the list that I get from virtual assistant).

This entails making sure there are no duplicates in my mailers, uploading my list to www.click2mail.com and inputting my list into RealProspect to track all my mailings. During this time period I might also work on my business systems, including creating five-minute videos to send my virtual assistants on how to find different lists and things like that. I might also spend this time writing new content for videos or researching new types of marketing.

The morning period is when I have no distractions, a lot of energy (after coffee), and feel like I can conquer the world. I like to do my creating in the morning at this elevated state and then turn to the managing of my business and systems in the afternoon when I have less energy and my attention level is slightly lower. Usually the rest of the morning is spent following up with old leads, responding to new leads, running comps, and updating my CRM system.

After lunch is when I normally would go out to visit any houses I am making offers on, checking on any rehab properties, and possibly meet with any other investors, real estate agents, or lenders. Evening time is usually when I do coaching and consulting calls with other investors looking to get into the off market business. Having a "to do" list each and every day is also very important to keep me focused.

Real Estate Stigmas

Within the real estate industry there are several stigmas associated with real estate professionals. Instead of pretending they don't exist I will address them right now.

Wholesalers

Over the last five or 10 years the wholesaling industry has gotten a bad name, and for good reason. There are a lot of great investors out there who understand how to ethically and legally wholesale deals and there are a lot of shady and unethical wholesalers out there doing deals the wrong way. Keep in mind if you tell someone that you are a wholesaler they may try to avoid working with you. In my opinion, wholesaling should be one of your exit strategies, but maybe not your first exit strategy.

You should be a real estate entrepreneur capable of being the agent on the deal, buying the deal yourself, or possibly passing on the deal as a wholesaler to your end buyer. Keep in mind that wholesaling happens all the time and if a real estate agent tells you it is illegal then they do not know what they are talking about. There are ways of doing any type of deal that could be illegal but wholesaling in and of itself is not illegal. Make it your goal to become a transaction engineer like I mentioned where you can utilize one of many strategies to buy or sell your deals.

Real estate agents

Many people in the investment and off market world see real estate agents as incompetent, lazy, too sales-focused, and any other number of other negative stereotypes. The reason for this probably comes because the barriers to entry for becoming a real estate agent are so embarrassingly low that anyone can become one these days.

If you are an agent (like myself) the best way to overcome people's hesitation is to be a professional in everything you do. For example, this would mean being up to date on the neighborhood, knowing the comps for the street, showing up on time, having a good understanding on contracts. Just those basic things alone will put you head and shoulders above most of the agents out there. Don't get me wrong there are a lot of amazing agents in the real estate field who are worth their weight in gold, but this section is focused on negative stereotypes.

Rehabbers Or Investors

Many people see rehabbers as chronic low-ballers who are only looking for a steal of a deal. While this may partly be true, if you are a rehabber you need to educate your agents and wholesalers on your exact criteria for buying.

You should give them an example deal analyzer calculator and let them know you are looking for a 15% return on any deal or you need to make at least $50,000 per rehab, or that you only buy in this area, etc. Many agents and wholesalers think that just because a property is listed as a foreclosure or listed in "as is" condition then it is a good deal. You need to teach your team better than that. Just keep in mind that there is sometimes a stigma with being a rehabber so if some agents don't want to work with you this should not offend you.

Do You Need An Office?

As you grow your off market business and real estate business in general you will start to consider getting an office as well as employees. I know people that do both and in this section I will go over the pros and cons of having an office versus doing everything virtually. For the investors that prefer to work from home, they typically have services like PAT Live or Answer First that screen all of their calls so that they don't need to hire a receptionist.

This allows the real estate entrepreneur to focus only on the high value, motivated sellers, because keep in mind most of your calls are not going to be from motivated sellers. If they are doing a rehab project they might have a project manager who handles site visits by looking at the different projects and then reporting back to the rehabber. This is a simple way of not really needing an office, however you still have to find a competent and trustworthy project manager. I also know some investors that do really well with having an office, employees, and more of a standard type of business set up.

Having an office is good to be able to leave your home and focus on business only. Sometimes people get distracted working from home. It is more of a preference and I would recommend trying both ways and see which you like better. There are many offices that you can lease short-term to try that arrangement.

Reputation Theory

Whether you are in a large city or small city the real estate community is a small world and word gets around quickly. You need to act in a way that builds your reputation for the future. Any time I am doing a deal whether it is an off market property or a listed property I do the deal as if I will be doing more deals with that agent. If you screw someone over, whether it is an agent or investor, keep in mind you will probably run into that person again.

That is why you want to be as straightforward and professional as possible as you can in any deal you do. I know plenty of agents and investors in my area that people love to work with based on their reputation and others that based on their reputation people want to avoid like the plague. I have worked with some amazing people over the years and at the same there are other people that I would never in a million years want work with again.

Even though the deal may have happened several years ago you are always going to remember an agent or investor who screwed you out of a commission or deal. Often times, when you are doing a deal, you want every variable that you can control going in your favor and sometimes just being on a good level with the other agent or investor and having done other successful transactions with them can get you the deal ahead of the next man or woman. Always keep in mind that you will see the same people over and over again, whether it's next week or two years from now, so act professionally!

Get In The Right State Of Mind

With real estate and in business you want to have every possible advantage. One of the best pieces of advice I can give you is to build a strong mental frame. This is not something you just wake up and say I'm going to have a strong mental frame. This is proactively doing several things so that your mindset is running optimally and when the inventible speed bumps along the road happen they won't derail you. The first part of having a strong mental frame is associating yourself with the right motivated, positive people.

Real estate is one business where you can find yourself with naysayers or sometimes just straight up losers that you want nothing to do with. I have realized that when I hang out with motivated, positive, people it just makes doing business much easier and more enjoyable. There was about a year I spent with a small real estate brokerage that was just barely getting by and I was associating with all of these people with closed off and scarcity mindsets. This would have derailed me if it was not for the massive amount of positive things I tried to include in my life. One example of what I did was to watch interviews with successful real estate professionals online. Watching just a couple of those every week or one every night had an incredibly powerful impact on my day-to-day and week-to-week business.

Reading books on motivation, mindset, and biographies are also great ways to build a strong mental frame. When you read the biography of someone like Cornelius Vanderbilt or some other tycoon of the era and see what they went through, you will have no issues whatsoever dealing with the mostly minor nonsense that can happen in real estate. You will realize that bouncing back is key to being successful and that is why I love biographies, you can see how famous moguls bounced backed from adversities.

To conclude there are three things that build a powerful mental mindset. The first is associating with the right people. Do not work with close-minded or negative people, there are enough people out there to not have anything to do with losers like that. I would recommend joining a high-level mastermind group where the people in the group are actually above you in their business. The second principle to building a strong mental mindset is the books you read. Make sure you read biographies of highly successful real estate people and others as well as motivational books and other business books that can assist you. The third strategy is listening to interviews from successful people.

I try to listen to at least one interview before I go to bed each night and really try to get inside the mindset of these millionaires and billionaires. If you are not proactive about building a strong mindset the metaphorical weeds will grow and you will start to take on negative habits and traits so be sure you are at least doing one of the three things I mentioned above.

Build A Treasure War Chest

I believe it was Dave Ramsey who first introduced me to the idea of the "treasure war chest." What he meant by this was in regards to personal finance, he talks about "piling up plunder" and building your treasure war chest to the point where you have enough in assets where nothing can really shake you. I interpreted his theory for the real estate business the same way. In building your real estate and off market business you should have set aside some savings and assets for that rainy day. You do not want to risk 100% of everything you own for the business. You should start buying a rental property or two here and there for the long term in addition to building up your savings and/or private lenders.

As you start your real estate business you should also be building your treasure war chest in terms of useful skills like learning direct mail marketing, learning online marketing, learning negotiating, and more because these skills are valuable in any industry. I would recommend every year or even every month you should have a new skill that you are adding, for example maybe one month you take a course on Google AdWords and you start with a small budget and start applying the lessons you learn. After several years these skills and assets that you are building up will pay off. You want do everything and anything you can to increase your value which then increases your earning ability.

Story

A while ago I was at a holiday party hosted by one of the top companies in my area that buys over 100 houses a year. I was just getting started in the off marketing business and wanted the real insider information on how the business worked and what I should be focusing on. They had their holiday party at a sports venue and let's just say that it was an open bar and everyone was having a great time. Toward the end of the night when everyone was basically hammered I started asking the CEO a lot of pointed questions about their marketing efforts. It turns out this company was spending tens of thousands of dollars each month getting qualified leads and they were getting over 500 leads each and every month.

He had also told me that the off market business is all about the marketing aspect because it generates the leads that result in completed deals. This was a perfect example of someone taking massive action and having massive success as a result. With 500 leads he could choose only the best, most profitable ones to work with and leave the rest of the leads for the birds. After that night I left super motivated, a little drunk, but with a crystal clear memory of everything he had said to me. Since then I have always looked at real estate in terms of scalability in relation to marketing and in terms of lead generation as the main priority.

Conclusion

These ideas I went over in this chapter is the accumulation of having spent years in the business and seeing what can go wrong as well as the best ways of doing business. A lot of my ideas come from modeling the best of the best, or in other words, none of my ideas are really that new. You don't need to apply every thing in this chapter, but typically the way it works in business is the more you apply the more results you get.

Action Item

I want you plan out what type of massive action you are going to take. You don't need to start out with thousands of letters or anything like that, but should have a three- and six-month plan of how you are going to scale up your marketing. I started by sending out a couple of hundred letters and eventually scaled up into the thousands. Sending out direct mail feels strange at first, but you will reach a point where you can send out 5,000 postcards in a month without even blinking.

I know one direct marketer who has sent a direct mail piece to one in six households in the United States. This was not for the real estate business but an example to illustrate the lengths some marketers will go to for leads. Some investors I know will tell me they put up to 10 bandit signs out and didn't get any leads, which does not surprise me. This is not thinking big. You need to be offending people with your marketing. Remember: if you haven't offended someone by noon each day with your marketing you are probably not doing enough of it. So get on it!

Also, if you have liked what you read so far I invite you to take the next step to get additional resources on the off market world including cool training videos, updates, live coaching, and more. All you have to do is text **OFFMARKET to 444999** to stay updated on everything going on in the off market world.

CHAPTER 8

Negotiating and Submitting Offers

Negotiation tactics in real estate is a topic of much debate that has seen hundreds of books written on it that promote a myriad of strategies. My opinion on negotiating is that each person is going to have their own style of communicating and they can all be successful, but there are some basics in each negotiation that you must know. Also keep in mind that you can improve each negotiation by looking back on any deal you did or any deal that got away and thinking about what you could do better next time.

Make It Simple and Easy

With motivated off market sellers they are looking for the easiest transaction possible. They realize that they can list the property on the MLS, have people walk through their house, and possibly have it sit on the market for a while. What you are offering is different. You are offering to either buy or bring the buyer for a fast close, "as is", with no real estate agent commission charged to the seller type of deal. In this case you want to emphasize how easy it will be for them to sell.

I will tell a couple of quick stories so you can see how this plays out in the real world of investing. One lady I was working with had gotten several postcards and wanted to get rid of her house as soon as possible. I was actually the second person she called. The first person for some reason wanted to partner with her as she fixed up the property and then they could both profit off of it. He provided her with a complex and detailed plan for this partnership, all of which confused the seller to no end. She called me exasperated from this other investor explaining all of this and told me she just wanted to sell as soon as possible in the current condition without listing it on the market. I made a simple (and lower) offer that met all of her needs and we closed on the property a couple of weeks later. The moral of that story is that a confused mind says no. Make things as simple as possible. The other investor lost out on a huge payday because they wanted to get fancy and structure this complicated deal when it didn't have to be that way and, more importantly, the seller didn't want that at all.

Another story I have deals with the paperwork. Some states are super bureaucratic and have like 50 pages of documents just to submit an offer. With off market deals I like to use two- or three-page contracts and make it as simple as possible for the seller to understand. The first deal I ever did was literally a one-page document that included the sale price, closing date, and a couple signatures. Now I don't recommend using that contract because some title companies probably would not approve it, but that was probably the easiest contract in the world to understand and was clear as can be. Make it as simple as possible for the seller to sell their house and when you talk to them listen to what they want (i.e. "I just want to get rid of the house") and give them what they want, which is usually a fast closing in the most hassle-free manner possible.

Gathering All The Information

When negotiating with sellers it always helps to have as much useful, relevant information as possible. Now I know that sounds obvious, but this is what I'm getting at: you need to have a seller interview sheet where you ask about things like address, condition, how many bedrooms/bathrooms, how soon they are looking to sell and how much they are looking for? This should help you to find out if it's a motivated seller or not.

Sometimes the property may have been listed in the past so you can look up that information on the MLS or Zillow to get an idea of the house including pictures, data, as well as the price it sold for. The only people you should be working with are motivated. If the seller says something like, "I want to sell in six months maybe, the house is in great condition, and we want to sell for $1M dollars," then it's probably not someone you want to spend your time on.

You are looking for the sellers that want to sell immediately, house needs a lot of work, and their price is realistic. Also, if you are bringing a buyer for this deal getting as much information as possible will help them evaluate the deal as well. Some sellers will want to tell you their life story over the phone so make sure you are not spending all day with a seller. Be courteous, professional, get the information you need, and then take that lead to the next step of evaluating if you think it has potential.

Start Lower Than You Can Pay

When making an offer you always want to start at lower than what you would normally want to pay for the house. This is because the seller might try to negotiate with you and bring you up a bit. A major key to making offers is to build as much rapport as you can with the seller. I have had sellers sell to me for no other reason than I was just courteous and the other investors they spoke with were rude or arrogant.

If possible you should make the offer in person and have your three-page contract in a manila folder or portfolio that you can bring along with you to the house. Sometimes the seller is out of state, etc so you will have to email or fax them the offer. In terms of contingencies you almost always want to have an inspection contingency that will read something along the lines of "this property is contingent upon buyer's partner's approval at any time before closing at the sole discretion of buyer's partner." Now this is basically an out clause that can allow you to escape the deal if it's overpriced.

That does not mean you should just go making offers all the time knowing you can get out. I have only had to use this clause once or twice when there were unexpected major repairs like foundation issues that I was not aware of until later in the process. It does help you sleep a little bit better at night though knowing that you can back out if you absolutely have to.

Starting Point

Where should your offer come in at? We have a whole chapter dedicated to making offers, but basically here is what you want to do. The rule of thumb to use is the MAO formula or after renovated value times 0.7 minus the cost of repairs. This is what most investors purchase homes at. If this property is in a very nice area or the value is over $300,000 sometimes it makes sense to go above the MAO formula, but I would always use your deal analyzer calculator to make sure you know exactly how much profit either you or your investor will potentially be making.

Another good rule of thumb is to make sure it is selling for less than it would if the house was listed with a real estate agent. Just because it is off market does not mean it's a good deal. I know one real estate agent who brags about how he bought an off market home. In reality it was an overpriced For Sale By Owner, which most of them are. Off market deals should almost always come with some type of discount, usually a significant one.

When working with sellers you want to figure out how much they are looking for and then don't be afraid to begin with a lower offer. I have even offered half of what the seller has been looking for in the past and actually got them down quite a bit on price after negotiations. If they are looking for retail value then they are probably not realistic, however it could be good negotiating practice to just let them know that the type of offer you are making is different from a real estate agent listing so we take a convenience discount out before making our offer for being such a hassle-free service.

Make Your Offer and Shut Up

So one of the best deals I ever bought involved negotiating with an out of state property owner. I had taken her through my lead interview sheet trying to get as much information about the property as possible. I had a very good idea of everything but price; she was refusing to give me the price she wanted for the house and instead told me she has a couple people interested and to just make an offer. I ran my numbers using the MAO formula and then went even a little bit lower since I was not able to get access to this property.

It was small though so even with a full gut renovation it was not going to need a ton of work. I called her back expecting her to reject my offer and the moment I gave her the price I was willing to offer she literally started laughing over the phone. Typically if you are not familiar with negotiation at that point you as the potential buyer might start stammering and improve the offer, but I took a different approach. I knew that in negotiating the first person who speaks usually loses so I kept my mouth shut waiting for her to say "no thanks but I'll be accepting a different offer." Instead, after what seemed like 30 minutes (it was probably only 30 seconds) she responded by saying "oh sorry my co-worker said something funny, yes that offer works, send me over the paperwork." I could not believe it and had to put the phone down because I was so excited. It was a good thing I had not changed my offer at all.

Moral of the story, in negotiating you give your number and then you shut up. You do not speak again until the seller responds. And also keep in mind just because the seller may say they are talking to other investors does not always mean they are and does not mean they are necessarily going to be shopping your deal either. Often times motivated sellers are looking for the easiest transaction not the highest price so make sure to build rapport and offer the most simple way out of that house for them.

Multiple Ways To Contact You

This may sound simple, but most people usually only have one way for their prospect to get in touch with them. Whenever possible I will have a minimum of four or five ways for someone to contact me, which is fairly easy with all the technology at our fingertips. They can email, call, text, listen to a free recorded message, fax, send snail mail, or even fill out a form on my website.

You never know exactly who will be getting your marketing piece and some people would rather gather a little bit of information before contacting you directly. Other prospects might be nervous talking on the phone or may lack computer skills. You want to make it as easy as possible for your customer and also give them the choice of method of contact to make them comfortable and eventually build a rapport. Some of your marketing pieces or ads might not have enough space for multiple forms of contact, however whenever possible you should implement this strategy.

Working With Home Inspectors

One idea that I have used in the past if I was unsure of any off market deal I would work with a home inspector. Now most off market or "as is" sales are not going to allow any home inspections, however what you can do is more of an informal walk through that should only take 30 minutes or so where the inspector looks for any major defects in the house. Most home inspections are going to cost you around $500, however if you just tell the inspector you are an investor and just want them to make sure there is nothing major wrong with the house, they will often cut their rate to just a couple hundred bucks or less.

Ideally you want to find an experienced home inspector who comes recommended. You don't know how many times we have used a home inspector who makes it seem as if the house is ready to crumble when really all it needs is some minor grading or repairs. I personally prefer to use a home inspector who used to build homes and can properly evaluate if a big potential issue with a house is fixable and if so roughly how much it might cost.

Sometimes issues that look big and dangerous are not as bad as they seem, but it takes a trained eye to discern the difference. An additional idea is to study to become a home inspector, get a couple books, take a few tests, and see if you can pass the test. I have actually taken a course and found it to be very helpful. Actually going to home inspections, reading through old home inspections, and talking with home inspectors is going to give you a much better understanding than any test but it is just an idea for you to consider. There are many online courses or books you can buy that are very inexpensive and very helpful. Until you have gained significant experience with this I suggest adding a trusted home inspector to your Dream Team.

Getting Out Of An Off Market Deal

If you find yourself stuck with an off market deal that you can't move and you promised the seller you would help them sell there are a few options for you. For starters if you put the property under contract to purchase with the intention of either wholesaling it, rehabbing it, or joint venturing and you can't find anyone willing to work with you here is what you do.

You should have a clause in all your contracts along the lines of "this offer is contingent on buyer's partner's approval at any time before closing, at the sole discretion of buyer's partner." This clause will typically allow you to back out of a deal if you really have to and you won't lose your earnest money deposit. Now this does not give you carte blanche to just put any property under contract knowing that you can back out however it should let you rest a little easier at night knowing in the worst-case scenario you could back out.

If a deal looks like it might not have the potential of closing, at the earliest possible time I would go back to the seller and let them know. I remember one deal specifically where I underestimated how much it would cost to remove a tree that had been pushing against a foundation wall.

Within a couple days of putting the property under contract and quickly realizing the repairs would be significantly more I went back to the seller and let her know. I told her I could still buy the property but at about $15,000 less than we originally talked about because one of the foundation walls was compromised. She actually agreed and we were able to salvage the deal. Bottom line is do not wait for the last minute to back out of a deal, try to re-negotiate and if you can, always include the inspection contingency clause that I mentioned above.

Rapport, Rapport, Rapport

When you go to meet an off market seller at a property your biggest goal should be to build rapport with them. You want them on your side from the get go. You should not be wearing a suit and tie since you do not want to intimidate the seller and often times these properties will need significant repairs and be in bad condition. Usually I like to wear a polo, khakis, and some comfortable, yet professional shoes. As you go through the house with them you can bring a notebook jotting down any repair items or even taking a few photos (if you ask them).

Keep in mind that this is their property and most of the time these houses are not going to be in good condition. You want to keep the tone more positive than negative and by that I mean you don't need to call out everything in the house that needs to be fixed. I have been into houses literally piled with garbage and came out of there with a smile complimenting the overall structure of the house. I usually like to walk through, make small talk and then end the walk through with an offer.

I will tell them a couple positive things (I like the neighborhood, the structure of the house is good) and then end it with letting them know that the property does need some work, we do this all the time, and here is our offer. Before going to the house you should run your comps and as you go through the property you should be coming up with your offer number. I always go to the house with a number in mind and then depending on how good or how bad the house is in person I can modify my offer from there. You should always have a manila folder in your car of some blank offers.

Story

The numbers have to work for you. One of the first deals I ever did the seller wanted 120K and he was very motivated however his price was on the high side. I stuck to my very conservative number and offered him 60K. We met at 92K, which turned out to be an amazing high equity deal for my investor and I. We also bought the house in the "as is" condition and even bought that house with tenants still living inside. The seller was thrilled that we got that property off of his back and we made a great profit.

Conclusion

Negotiating offers is an important part of real estate and there is a strategy behind it. Number one, I only make offers to motivated sellers. I know some people that make 50 offers a week or something like that which in my mind is crazy. They make offers to anyone and everyone. Pretty much the only offers I make are to QUALIFIED people who have identified themselves are motivated, their house as needing work, and with a realistic asking price. This will save you a lot of headache by only negotiating with motivated sellers. For the super motivated sellers, even if their asking price is not realistic I will still make them an offer just because of their level of motivation, but that is an exception, not the rule. Remember to make the offer and then be quiet!

Action item

Practice your seller interview sheet while keeping in mind that you want to be building rapport with the seller. You do not want to just read through the sheet like a robot. Some sellers will not call anyone else if they get along with you, trust you, and you give them a fair offer. You can print it out and practice the seller interview sheet for 30 minutes a day until you have it memorized. Keep in mind to try and keep the calls under five minutes or so because your time is valuable, too. Some sellers will talk your ear off and it's important to just get the basic information and move on with the process or on to the next lead. There will be a lot of leads out there. If you have a friend or business associate you can practice the seller interview sheet with them a few times a day to make you more comfortable.

Also, if you have liked what you read so far I invite you to take the next step to get additional resources on the off market world including cool training videos, updates, live coaching, and more. All you have to do is text **OFFMARKET to 444999** to stay updated on everything going on in the off market world.

CHAPTER 9

Alternative Real Estate Investing ideas

In this chapter we are going to cover some additional ideas when it comes to real estate investing and off market deals. There are a lot of alternative theories out there some that work great and others not so much. This chapter should get you thinking in different ways than you are used to and can make you better at spotting lucrative investments.

Starbucks Effect

I believe Zillow were the first ones to research the concept of the Starbucks effect. If you are looking for a house to appreciate in value, you should look for a Starbucks coffee shop. According to Zillow's research, between 1997 and 2013 those homes closer (within a quarter of a mile) to Starbucks increased in value by 96% compared to 65% for other homes.

In general, these homes near a Starbucks are probably going to be more expensive, however they will also appreciate faster than your typical home. Further studies have been done that indicate that upward prices follow the arrival of a Starbucks and this effect is not limited to timing and location. There are probably several reasons behind this.

One of them being that Starbucks has very large cash reserves and can pay the top analytics experts in the world to sort through the myriad of factors used in picking the neighborhoods with the most potential for growth. Another factor is that people tend to want to live near amenities including restaurants, cafes, and more. It is even more desirable for these amenities to be located within walking distance or close by.

Zillow also found a similar correlation of appreciating value on homes located near a Dunkin Donuts location, although it was not as strong as that related to Starbucks. When in doubt, do not be swayed by the know-it-all real estate agent who is giving you 1,000 reasons why you should or should not buy in one neighborhood, trust in the analytics experts at Starbucks who specifically chose the new location for a good reason. Your decision should be even easier if there are multiple Starbucks locations in close proximity to the property you are considering.

Whole Foods Effect

In terms of off market properties, investing in real estate, and picking up on trends the "Whole Foods effect" has been a much discussed topic. This ties into the Starbucks effect, although the relationship between a Whole Foods and appreciating property values may be stronger since a high-end supermarket is a larger investment than a coffee shop. Zillow wrote about this principle in their popular book "New Rules of Real Estate" which I would highly recommend you check out.

The idea is pretty simple, and states that if a Whole Foods moves into your neighborhood the property values will increase at a higher rate than those without a Whole Foods or neighborhoods farther away from the Whole Foods. Zillow conducted a study from 1997 to 2014 on homes near Whole Foods and Trader Joes. Homes located within a mile of either type of store were worth more than twice as the median home in the United States.

One could make the argument that the store just picks the right neighborhoods that are set to appreciate or that the actual Whole Foods causes the appreciation, but either way the result is the same: it seems it would be wise to invest for the long term near a Whole Foods. Keep in mind that Whole Foods is a billion dollar corporation, like Starbucks, that pays some of the best and brightest in the industry to study where their next location should open up. It would be wise to follow their suggestions.

Gayborhoods

Now I have to be careful what I say in regards to fair housing laws with "gayborhoods," but again this is not my theory and I will do my best to be politically correct. This is what Zillow has to say about "gayborhoods": if you buy in a neighborhood that receives this description your house will appreciate more than in a non-"gayborhood." Zillow did a 40-year study and found that "home prices in historically gay neighborhoods have steadily outperformed average prices for the metros in which they're located." Zillow looked at neighborhoods around the country and chances are if you live near a big city you have probably witnessed it first hand, although you may not be aware.

I will not speculate as to why "gayborhoods" appreciate so much more, but 40 years of evidence from a legitimate source is enough evidence for this real estate professional. So, if you are looking for an off market deal that has a lot of potential for appreciation, find the "gayborhood," buy there, and hold on to that piece of property. Better yet, buy an off market house in a "gayborhood", next to a Whole Foods and with a Starbucks nearby. If you work the deal correctly, you could potentially retire off of it. To find the best up and coming "gayborhoods" you could talk to your network, do online research or read the gay-friendly magazines, since each city usually has one. Overall, the idea is to find the next hotspot!

Pocket Listings?

Pocket listings have also become very popular in recent times. The way a pocket listing works is that in an exclusive type of neighborhood or high-end market an agent might privately look to a sell a house without actually putting in on the MLS. This is usually different than an off market deal because most pocket listings are on the extremely high end of the market and although they are not listed, they typically do not come with any type of discount like the off market deals I have been talking about in this book.

Agents will do pocket listings to have more privacy, security, and create a sense of scarcity. It could be good for you as a buyer since theoretically there will be less eyes on the property and therefore less bidders. However, what I have found is that these listings are typically much higher in price and usually do not come with a discount. Sometimes real estate agents keep a listing as a pocket listing so that they can get both sides of the commission. They are a something I would keep an eye on because I have seen high-end pocket listings become more and more popular, however you are typically not going to get any type of discount with these houses since they are already so highly priced.

Crowdfunding

Crowdfunding has become a big business recently and has even spread out to the real estate industry where there are some hot startups like FundRise and RealtyMogul among others. In terms of getting your off market deal financed I still think the best source of funds is going to be your local hard moneylender or private money that you borrow from an investor.

If you have some extra cash that you are looking for a good potential return on then crowdfunding could be exactly what you are looking for. I love the idea of crowdfunding for real estate and it is certainly something to keep your eye on, however for most residential off market investment opportunities, they need to be funded in less than 30 days with no strings attached. I think right now many of the crowdfunding real estate investment opportunities are for commercial properties that have longer closing time frames.

The best off market deals typically only last for 24-48 hours before an investor puts them under contract and then they need to close fast soon after. As a real estate professional you should do some research into crowdfunding and be knowledgeable about the subject.

Is The Market Going Up Or Down?

Predicting the real estate market is almost impossible. I would have to refer to legendary economist Burton Malkiel who published the book "A Random Walk Down Wall Street" and made the argument that a "blindfolded monkey throwing darts at a newspapers financial pages could select a portfolio that would do just as well as one carefully selected by the stock experts." Upon further due diligence it was discovered that Makiel did not give enough credit to the monkeys. About 80% of fund managers have failed to beat the S&P 500 year in and year out. People that are paid hundreds of thousands and sometimes millions of dollars per year cannot actually beat the average market return. There are very few stock experts that can consistently beat the average market returns of the S&P 500 and I believe the same to be true with real estate.

The market will go up or down, but either way it is going to be near impossible to predict the rate and frequency of change. There are real estate cycles that some argue happen every 10 or 20 years, however in each city you will have a different outcome. My overall strategy is to look for undervalued properties relative to what others in the neighborhood are selling for (off market) at the given time and also I would rely on Zillow's recommendations like looking for properties near Whole Foods, Starbucks, and gayborhoods that have long term appreciation value.

Auction Homes

Depending on what part of the country you are in, auctions could be a good source of off market deals. For example in Maricopa County (Phoenix, Arizona area) a couple times every week you will see tons of people down at the courthouse steps bidding on auction homes. They even have donuts, bring coffee, and have huge balloons. A television series was made about the auctions down there. They auction off tons of foreclosures every week. However, other areas across the country there may only be 10 or so properties at auction on a given day and maybe only two or three will actually sell.

I would recommend checking out the auctions in your area for the experience, however keep in mind you typically have to fund them with your own cash in a very short closing period and in almost every case you will not be able to go inside the property before making an offer. This means that you will have to estimate any repair costs and hope for the best. Auctions are great places to meet other investors although keep in mind sometimes they just want to focus on the auction and as such may not be the friendliest people.

You will meet all different types of people at an auction from beginners, to grizzled vets and these people could be good buyers for you for some of your other deals. The top investment companies that I know typically do not buy at auctions. That being said, everyone has his or her own niche and if you learn the auction system better than anyone else you can gain a competitive advantage and get it to work for you. Some companies are even developing software and programs that let you bid on auction properties without actually going to the courthouse, they have bidders that will bid by proxy for you. If you are a savvy buyer and know exactly what you are looking for and willing to do some repair work, this could be a great option.

My Opinion On Zillow

Everyone has an opinion on Zillow and here is mine. I think Zillow, like most things in life, is good and bad, it just depends on the situation. If you are starting out as a real estate entrepreneur and you do not have access to the MLS then I think Zillow is a great resource. You can look at properties, do research on your neighborhood and get a good sense of prices out there.

Additionally, when you are running comps on any house you can use Zillow as a rule of thumb. One thing I did when I was first starting out was if I had a motivated seller I would find out what price they were looking for and then I would compare that to the Zillow value. If there was a big difference between those two prices then I knew that the deal had potential. However, all things being considered I believe the MLS to be best resource. The MLS is going to have the most up-to-date and accurate information. Sometimes the Zillow values are all over the place and can give the sellers an inflated price for the value of their home.

You can rely on Zillow when you are getting started, but as soon as you possibly can you should try to get MLS access by getting your real estate license. Zillow also has a feature called "make me move" where you can find out the price a seller is willing to sell for in your area and even contact them about selling. This is good practice when you are starting out and can make you more comfortable interacting with sellers. One thing to watch out for with Zillow is their "pre-foreclosure" part of their website.

In my experience what happens is that someone might have missed or been late on a payment a year or two ago, however Zilllow's data will show the property as currently being in foreclosure. You will see tons of fake preforeclosure listings on Zillow. Overall though, the company Zillow as a whole seems to be an innovative, forward thinking company and I would recommend checking out the book they published "The New Rules of Real Estate" which has some very interesting ideas in it, some of which I mention in this book.

Does AirBnB work?

Airbnb is an interesting concept and is one that is evolving on a day-to-day basis as the service grows in popularity. Since I do not actively have any off market deals or any properties that I rent out with Airbnb this is what I would say about it.

Some people make a killing off of this service, often times in big cities where a hotel might be sold out or way too expensive.

I would try to look into doing Airbnb, however I probably would not buy a condo with the idea that you are going to make it a full-time Airbnb suite. Many condos and apartments are cracking down on people that rent out their units and I have even heard of fines being issued for repeat offenders. You should never ask a condo board or a property management company if they allow Airbnb, the answer will always be "no." However, keep in mind plenty of people still rent their units out and find ways to do it. If you have a house or a town home, the restrictions might be less if there are any at all. I know of one client we worked with who was just a couple miles from a big city and bought the house with the idea he was going to turn his basement into an Airbnb suite.

The first thing I would do if I were to consider this proposition is read every single article available about AirBnB, ranging from the horror stories to the people making six figures on properties they don't even own. I think you can develop a strategy upon doing a little research so you can get a better understanding of the business. As always, if you have any doubts make sure to consult a legal professional. It is an extremely popular service and there is potential if you want to rent out different rooms so I would look into it for sure.

Foreclosure Homes

Depending on what city you live in, maybe its Phoenix, Detroit, or the entire state of Maryland you may have a lot of foreclosure properties. These are typically not going to be off market because they will be listed with an REO (bank owned) real estate agent. As an off market specialist, I do not typically work with foreclosures because they are rarely "off market" unless you want to consider auction properties which we talked about earlier.

Some investors I know like to reach out to any agent that has listed a foreclosure property recently and to let them know about any upcoming deals and this could certainly be a good strategy. Often times the banks are just trying to unload these houses and if you can be the first one in there with a good offer your chances are much better. Some people I know also try to contact the sellers in pre-foreclosure where you can mail them letters or door knock and try to get a deal that way. Each state is different in regards to pre-foreclosure laws and regulations in terms of contacting sellers so for the most part this is one niche that I have stayed away from.

I prefer to market to the high-equity, often times absentee-owned properties because I have just found the process to be much easier than dealing with banks, evictions, and everything that come along with foreclosures. If you have a good understanding of the foreclosure process and some type of competitive advantage then by all means go for the foreclosure market. Everybody has his or her niche and I encourage you to find yours!

Should I Make Offers On FSBOs?

When I talk about off market deals I do NOT mean FSBOs. FSBOs are some of the most non-motivated sellers out there and I will tell you a quick story about why. When I was young and broke in the real estate business I ran a service that listed people's houses for a very low cost. The rationale was based on advice from my broker at the time. He told me was that after a year I could tell people in my first year that I sold 100 million or some crazy number like that, even though the only service I was providing was adding the property to the MLS. Over the course of the year I had about 100 houses and only about 30% sold, which is not a good return, especially when one considers the hot real estate market that I was in.

It is comical to hear FSBOs talk about why their house is worth $50,000 more than the price at which every other house listed has sold. Sometimes they would even call me and ask why I thought their house was not selling or, better yet, why no one has contacted them. Many times the seller would call me thinking I had put the wrong contact information into the MLS because they had not gotten any response or calls. While trying to be nice I would politely tell them that their house was overpriced compared to what any other house had sold for and that they would have to bring the price down to get any action. Most of them would not heed my advice. If I were you I would avoid FSBOs like a bad cold. They are oftentimes some of the most unrealistic people out there.

Story

In this chapter I gave a lot of ideas on where you should buy and in these next paragraph or two I will tell you where you should NOT buy. There are some types of purchases that I would stay away from. I remember a while back there was what we like to call the "know-it-all" buyer. Not surprisingly they had just gotten rid of the house they had owned for about 10 years and barely broke even, although the neighborhood had appreciated significantly in that time, they had just bought it completely wrong.

They wanted to now buy a house in one certain neighborhood although they could not really find anything good in their price range. So, what they ended up doing was buying a house listed on the market (so they did not get any type of discount) across from that particular neighborhood directly in front of a school, on a double yellow lane road (i.e. tons of traffic), and not only that but the only other offer was a slightly lower one and was from a builder (this house was barely livable). When you think of re-sale value and appreciation you need to take into account the fact that many people will be turned off by living directly in front of a school, on a busy road, in tear-down condition, and close to the ideal neighborhood but technically not in the good area.

I am curious what the exit strategy will be for this seller down the road, my guess is that it will have to sell to a builder for the price of the land since the house is so old and dilapidated. But not only that, many builders may not even want to touch that house since a busy road or being in front of a school could easily force them to drop their price significantly from other properties in the same neighborhood.

Conclusion

Everyone has their own theories on real estate and in this chapter I tried to address most of the major ideas and investing strategies out there. I believe that everyone in real estate has their own niche and I would recommend to look more into these different strategies and see what more you can learn about them. When you buy real estate you need to think of your long term value and some of the ideas I mentioned are statistically proven to appreciate more so than other types of purchases.

Action Item

Go to the library or Amazon.com and buy Zillow's New Rules of Real Estate. That book goes more in depth on various investment strategies, real estate information, and much more. Just by reading that book you will probably know more than many real estate professionals out there.

Also, if you have liked what you read so far I invite you to take the next step to get additional resources on the off market world including cool training videos, updates, live coaching, and more. All you have to do is text **OFFMARKET to 444999** to stay updated on everything going on in the off market world.

CHAPTER 10

Real Estate Education, Certifications, and Mentorship

In real estate there are a lot of certifications and educational programs out there. Some certifications cost $100 and others are quite a bit more expensive. Here are my thoughts on certifications and if you need them for your off market career. I think as a real estate entrepreneur doing off market and on market deals you should always be learning, taking classes, and improving yourself.

What I have found is that while a lot of these certifications are helpful there are not necessarily going to teach you as much as you think. Getting your hands dirty and actually doing deals is the best way to improve yourself as a real estate professional. Some people I know like to brag about all the alphabet soup they have behind their name and it is one thing if you are a doctor, lawyer, or MBA but taking a two-day online real estate course is easy.

You should be bragging (if at all) about all the deals you have done and all the experience you have. When it comes to certifications, you should certainly try to attain them if you have the time and money, but don't it make it your number one focus. Your priority should be on getting leads for your business, converting those, and improving what you can for the next deal.

Should You Get A Real Estate License?

Okay, the age old question, should you get your real estate license or not? I would highly recommend getting your license. Just about every real estate entrepreneur I know has his or her real estate license and it can open the door for you literally and figuratively. The most important part of getting your real estate license is that you have access to the MLS which is going to give you access to all the active homes, recently sold properties, and under contract houses in your area, in addition to a wealth of other information.

In this day and age, it is not enough to rely just on Redfin or Zillow for your comps. A second reason to get your license is so that you can do deals as an agent. Once you start marketing for off market opportunities you are going to come across sellers who would be better served by using a real estate agent on their property. Whether it is you just bringing a buyer or it is you listing their home, you will come across sellers that need your services and you should be prepared when you do. Keep in mind, getting your real estate license is not extremely difficult. It is actually shockingly easy to get your real estate license and is not very expensive either.

There are plenty of online courses you can take to prepare and it should not take you more than a month or so to get ready for your test. You can also retake the test multiple times if you fail. If for whatever reason you really just don't want to be licensed what you can do is have your significant other get their real estate license so that at least one of you has access to the MLS and can list houses if necessary. Some investors prefer to be strictly an investor and they don't want to have to disclose to the seller that they are an agent so they don't end up getting their license. I have never had a seller back out of a deal I was buying because I told them I was an agent, however it could be a valid concern.

John Carlton Advice

One of my favorite marketing strategists and legends in their own right is a guy named John Carlton and he said, "you cannot take advice from anyone who hasn't actually been there." This applies directly to the off market real estate world and the real estate investing world in general.

Having been directly involved in both worlds for the last five years or so you will hear all types of strange and bizarre theories, tips, and ideas from people who have not done a single thing in either the off market world or the investment world. To me it is almost insane how willing and able people with almost zero experience in both worlds will routinely give out advice as if they had been doing this stuff for the last 30 years.

You need to only listen to successful people that are actively involved in the off market and investment world. My best recommendation for this if you cannot find anyone local is to listen to as many interviews and podcasts on places like BiggerPockets, FlipNerd and many other sites out there. Do not take what your local "know-it-all real estate agent" has to say about a topic at face value, often times they are only dealing with retail clients who buy traditional houses, not people working in the off market world.

Dan Kennedy Advice

Here is a theory from one of my favorite authors, mentors, and business strategists alive, Dan Kennedy. Any endeavor you undertake including finding off market deals and just being in the real estate industry in general you should seek to accumulate mass information. Dan Kennedy says one of the differences between the "renegade millionaires" he works with as clients and others is that his renegade millionaires tend to go into mass accumulation mode of information when they start something.

For the off market industry this would mean looking online for those that are already successful in the off market world, reading their story, listening to their interviews, digging up as much information as possible about them. Most people, Dan Kennedy says, usually only go into "mass accumulating of information mode" when they or someone they know are diagnosed with a disease. Although this sounds bad, you need to go in to the off market world with that kind of mindset looking for any useful pieces of information that can assist you in this business.

Personally, I have probably listened to hundreds of interviews of the top investors and off market guys in the business taking notes, doing research on them, and really trying to figure out what the commonalities were in all their successes. I have read books by all the top investors and read articles online, to learn how these different investors and agents got started in the business.

More often than not the main commonality is that they discovered mass marketing and action taking. It always shocks me how little most people in the real estate industry know about the history of their business, the major players in their business, or even that there are various exit strategies available. By listening to interviews you can learn the mistakes to avoid and also pick up some great tips that can help you reach the next level.

Real Estate Scam Or Education?

You have probably seen the ads or know people who have spent thousands of dollars on real estate related seminars, mentorship, and education. Is it worth it? The short answer is: Yes! If you don't pay up front to learn from the best then I can guarantee you that you will pay on the back end when one of your deals goes sour. I've seen it first hand countless times. My belief is that for whatever reason most people reach a certain level where they stop learning.

They might be fairly successful and think that there is nothing else to really master. This is a false narrative. If you can find a good real estate education program they can often show you better ways of doing things you have done in the past and perhaps help you reach that next level in your career. And remember, there is always a next level. I know a lot of people who scoff at the idea of paying thousands of dollars for a real estate program. However keep in mind, if you spend thousands of dollars on some program and just learn one thing that you can implement with your deals, which can easily pay for the course itself, oftentimes within the first deal.

Real estate is a high income, high stakes profession and in my opinion you should be willing to pay for whatever tools and skills you need to learn to get to the next level. It is funny because I know one agent and investor who has over 400 people in his organization, has a business with over $100 million in revenue, could retire tomorrow with tens of millions, yet he still goes to seminars, pays coaches, reads, learns, and implements new things every day.

At the same time I know a real estate agent who has about 5 agents in his brokerage and believes he is above any real estate coaching or training. Yes, real estate education is expensive, but what is more expensive is not knowing or understanding something that leads to leaving money on the table or missing out on a deal because you did not know the next steps to take.

I know some of the top investors in the country who routinely pay tens of thousands of dollars a year to different coaches, consultants, and others to try to help them step their business up even further. Some people who have been trained in the more traditional formal education way would scoff at the idea of paying for a real estate program. However, what they often fail to consider is the specialized knowledge required in the real estate business. Most people don't know this but many of the top residential real estate investors got started with some type of coaching program or system to give them a framework in the beginning. Every dollar that you invest in coaching is an investment in yourself and your business that can and, I believe, will reap large benefits for you and your business.

Story

You should always try to educate yourself with new books, certifications, courses, whatever it may be but at the same time don't take yourself too seriously and keep in mind real world experience is usually going to win.

I worked with one person who had gotten a Master's degree in something that sounded interesting but I was not sure exactly how that degree would help them in the real world. Because of this degree, they thought they knew everything about everything and it was very difficult to work with them. They had never gotten their hands dirty in real estate deals or small business so their communication skills were very poor. Emails were very long, verbal communication was overly formal as if you presenting a case to the United Nations, and not only that they always wanted to have meetings, sometimes lasting hours.

I guess the moral of the story is to always be educating yourself, but more important than that is actual real world experience and never take yourself too seriously whether you have one certification or degree, or if you have all of them. Strive for a combination of books smarts while also having street smarts and real world experience. Or in other words, do not act like an entitled millennial, you must work hard, treat every day like you are the intern, and stay humble.

Conclusion

I highly believe in educating yourself and more importantly finding mentors that can assist you. Sometimes you need to pay for these mentors or other times you can even work for them. Every year I lay out an education goal in terms of how many books I want to read, seminars I want to take, and new skills I want to learn. The best investors I know are always evolving and I would recommend you do the same.

Action Item

Find a mentor. I would recommend that you pay for one as well. The reason behind paying for a mentorship type of program is that you will value it so much more. The program I paid for was very expensive and as a result I would stay up nights studying the course, implementing the material, and it paid off for me in a short period of time and still pays off to this day. Every time someone gives me a course or something for free it is never my first priority.

I recently gave a friend this amazing audio program that was not cheap. She had begged and begged me for it and a couple weeks after giving it to her I asked her about it. She had listened to 30 minutes of it and then said it was not any good and I can guarantee you it was because she got it for free. She had been desperate for it and now nothing. If she had paid for it she would have placed a lot more value on the program and would have listened to it. It reminds me when I had begged a very successful investor to give me his course for free and then after receiving it I may have spent about 10 minutes on it before moving on. I had no appreciation for it since I did not spend any hard earned money on it. If you are too cheap for a mentor or don't want to make a big commitment a great FREE place for "mentors" is YouTube videos where they interview different real estate professionals. You can learn so much on those interviews and there are literally thousands freely available on YouTube.

Also, if you have liked what you read so far I invite you to take the next step to get additional resources on the off market world including cool training videos, updates, live coaching, and more. All you have to do is text **OFFMARKET to 444999** to stay updated on everything going on in the off market world.

CHAPTER 11

Resources For Your Off Market Business

There are numerous great websites out there that you can use as resources for the off market business and I will talk about some of my favorites for finding off market deals and keeping up to date with the industry:

Biggerpockets.com

In my opinion, this is the go-to site for real estate investing, finding off market deals, and more of the creative side of the business. You will find all different types of articles, audio, video on marketing for off market deals, structuring off market deals, and you can even connect with other investors in your local area. I would be sure to check out their interviews on their YouTube channel. You can gain incredible insight into how different investors across the United States are finding such great off market deals. On their forums, you can also connect with like-minded real estate professionals in your own backyard.

Flipnerd.com

Is another great resource for finding off market deals across the country, finding the best vendors to build your local dream team in real estate, and networking with other professionals. They also have amazing interviews on there with some of the top off market experts from around the US. With the interviews you have the option to listen to the audio or read the transcript if that's what you prefer. In one day you could probably go through every interview transcript picking up and highlighting the best business idea or two that you hear from each interview. This has the potential to completely transform your business and mindset. Flipnerd is similar to BiggerPockets and I would recommend checking both sites out.

Inman.com

The Inman news website is a great site for the real estate industry overall and will keep you up to date with the topics of the day. It does not necessarily focus on off market deals, however there are a lot of interesting articles written by people in all parts of the real estate industry to give you a good perspective. They will cover new trends, real estate apps, market news, and much more. Also, each year they have conferences where they give out awards for new and innovative business ideas related to real estate.

Synch Your Various Real Estate Sites

One thing I like to do as well is for all the local real estate news in my area I use the Feedly iPhone app that syndicates multiple local real estate sites so I can cross-reference them. This helps so that you are not going all around the Internet trying to track down the real estate news of the day. If you have a break in the day or you are waiting on someone you can check your app and get caught up on all the local real estate news fairly quickly. Any time you are talking with a client or seller and you can talk about what is currently going on directly in that neighborhood makes you sound like the expert and enhances your credibility. I would add about 5-10 local real estate websites to that app so you can stay up to date on neighborhood and national real estate news.

Keep in mind there are many more great sites out there, but this should get you started and keep you busy reading and listening to these site's material for a while.

Real Estate Apps That You Must Have For the Off Market Business

Here are five real estate apps that I like to use for off market deals and the real estate business in general. Every month there also seem to be some cool new real estate app that comes out, so keep your eyes and ears opened.

Deal Analyzer App

You should have some type of deal analyzer app on your phone where it is basically just a calculator but takes into account closing costs, holding time, renovations, etc. I use the Fortune Builders App which is freely available to download, however there are other options out there.

PDF Converter App

Did you know you can turn a photo or jpeg image into a PDF instantly and for free? There are now plenty of apps available where you can take a photo on your phone and with the app turn it into a PDF that you can print out, edit, and/or send to a title company or buyer. I use an app called Genius Scan and there are many others widely available.

Feedly App

Although I mentioned this earlier, this is one of my favorite apps because it gets me caught up on all the real estate news happening in my local area. The way it works is you just copy and paste and links to real estate blogs, websites, or local news sites and every day it will give you an updated list of all the real estate news from the links you included. I have about 10 different sites that I read for real estate and community information and this app allows me to get caught up on everything in my down time while I am waiting at a property, getting car serviced, drinking a coffee, etc.

Audible

I love having this app/service because for $15 a month or so I can listen to an audiobook about real estate, biography, mindset, or whatever it may be on various speed levels. This service allows you to listen to books on 1.5X, 2X, or even 3X speed so that you can finish books quickly and even listen to them several times. When you are driving to properties or sitting in traffic this is a great app to have. I look forward to long drives now because I know I will be getting smarter.

Redfin

This is another free app that can show you all the active, sold, under contract properties in your area. If you want to pull up comps and drive the neighborhood you can see which houses sold for what price and also pull up the actual listing as well.

I would advise starting with these apps and then expanding from there. This is not an exhaustive list and I'm sure new apps are being built as you read this. A bonus tidbit about my recommendations is just about all of them are free!

Recommended Reading and Why

Here are the top three books I would recommend for learning marketing, the off market business, and setting up consistent and scalable systems.

No B.S. Direct Marketing by Dan Kennedy. If you have not ready anything by or heard of Dan Kennedy this is someone you need to follow. Although this book is not real estate specific it applies to any type of local business and also gives you ideas on evolving your current business to the next level.

A lot of his business ideas are counterintuitive to what you would learn in a business class or any type of traditional advice that people give. There are countless entrepreneurs that credit Dan Kennedy with being the main reason that they became millionaires (and I hope to be one of them soon). He has additional books and courses that I would recommend. Ever since I read No B.S. Direct Marketing my business and outlook has never been the same.

The E-myth Revisted by Michael Gerber. This book is great because it is all about creating scalable, repeatable systems for your business. The E-myth shows you how to go from the "technician," which is where most small business owners are, to the manager and progress all the way up to the entrepreneur. This book shows you how to create a franchise-like system for your business no matter what industry you are in. It is a relatively quick read and something I would recommend reading several times.

The Millionaire Real Estate Agent by Gary Keller. This is an amazing book for real estate agents as well as other real estate professionals looking to build their business. The Millionaire Real Estate Agent was written by one of the founders of Keller Williams (Gary Keller) and goes through the systems, mindsets, and strategies of million dollar earners across the country. Probably the best thing about this book is the profiles of different agents, how they build their teams, marketing, and their story of how they got started in real estate all the way to reaching their current level of success.

These three books are the ones I have found to be most practical and helpful in getting started with my off market real estate career. The books will set a good foundation for you moving forward and I would not stop with those. Continue to read and learn as much as you can. I like to read a book a week on a new subject because you never know where your next great idea is going to come from! It is also very useful to learn from people who have already been and there and done that so that you can model exactly what they did to become successful.

Additional Resources

Real Estate Deal Analyzer
http://bit.ly/2dcJwQW

Repair Estimator
www.homeadvisor.com

Direct Mail Fulfillment Companies

www.click2mail.com
www.yellowletterscomplete.com

Live Phone Answering Services

www.PATlive.com
www.answerfirst.com

CHAPTER 12

It Is Your Turn to Start Doing Off Market Deals.

By reading this book you now have everything you need to start doing off market deals no matter if you are an investor, Real estate agent, or bargain hunter, these strategies work for anyone who applies the strategies I teach.

If you diligently follow what I've laid out in this book you will start finding high equity deals that nobody else even knows are for sale. You can buy them for yourself, sell them to an investor, or even work out partnerships with other local real estate professionals.

Follow this blueprint exactly whose strategies have already helped over 1000 off market deal hunters around the US sharpen their marketing skills for off market real estate deals.

The next step is all on you.

Take massive action. Make a commitment, at the very least, of six months to implement as many of these strategies as possible. Decide that you will do at least one deal over the course of the next year. All you need is 50 leads (on average), if you want to break that up into a month-by-month basis that is literally only one lead a week.

The only reason I am sharing this information on off market deals is because I truly enjoy coaching and mentoring and I have seen a lot of misinformation out there on how to find off market deals and I wanted to set the record straight from someone who has been in the business his entire business career.

Happy deal hunting!

Thank you for downloading my book! I invite you to follow me on my various networks so that you can stay with me as I travel through the world of off market real estate deals.

Instagram: @j_late12

Snapchat: jrl560

Facebook: https://www.facebook.com/jeff.leighton.5

Also, if you have liked what you read so far I invite you to take the next step to get additional resources on the off market world including cool training videos, updates, live coaching, and more. All you have to do is text **OFFMARKET to 444999** to stay updated on everything going on in the off market world.

Also, feel free to shoot me an email at my personal address at JRLeighton12@gmail.com. I love hearing feedback on my content and I will try to answer every email that I get.

I appreciate all of your feedback and would love to hear what you have to say so that I can make my next version even better.

Please leave me a helpful REVIEW on Amazon by turning the page.

Thanks!

-Jeff Leighton

www.ingramcontent.com/pod-product-compliance
Lightning Source LLC
Chambersburg PA
CBHW031054180526
45163CB00002BA/836